Social Security & Medicare Benefits Guide
Solving the Puzzle

B.J. Elgin

Social Security & Medicare Benefits Guide: Solving the Puzzle
By B.J. Elgin
www.bbbenefitsguru.com

ISBN 978-1-7326758-0-3

Copyright © 2019

Vale Summit Press

Disclaimer
The information in this book pertains to benefit programs administered only within the United States and should in no way substitute for financial or legal advice. It is impossible to outline all the variables in the types of benefits administered by Social Security. This guide is intended to provide essential information for the most common benefit applications. The federal agencies which oversee the programs covered in this book should be consulted regarding details for your specific situation.

Acknowledgements

I wish to thank the following people:

Elisabeth Stuckey - without her assistance this guide would
never have made it to print.

Helane DiGravio, Barbara Linthicum, and Katrina Eversole whose expertise and
review of the subject matter affirmed my desire to publish this guide.

Kathy Long, Donna Mason,
Elaine Rose, Nancy Souders, Kelly Swisher,
Peggy Swisher, Cindy Wallace, Marisa Young,
whose assistance as proofreaders
and encouragement kept me moving toward the goal.

Shary Green, Seth Howard and Josh Youngbar
who lent their unique talents to help me "get the job done."

and finally, my husband, Dan Elgin, who proofread this guide many times
and encouraged me to not give up. I am grateful.

Thank you to the cover models:

Oliver Blevins, Aidan Elgin, Katrina Eversole, Dawn Lowenhaupt,
Ana Martinez, Carl Thomas, and Cheng (Kevin) H. Zheng

Cover Design by Josh Youngbar

Dear Reader,

Most of us never think about Social Security until we need it. Then begins the search for answers. What kind of benefits am I eligible for? When can my benefits start? How much will I get? Can I work and still get benefits? Can my family get benefits? Can I get Medicare? So many questions. Where do I get the answers? How do I make sense of it all?

During my 31-year career with Social Security and seven years in senior services, and in the many seminars and workshops I have led, I heard these questions many times. Someone once said to me that Social Security and Medicare seemed like a big jigsaw puzzle to them – with lots of pieces but no picture of how they all fit together. That is why I designed this guide in a format that lays out each type of benefit in its own chapter. I explain the qualifications for each type of benefit, how each type of benefit is figured, when and how to file for your benefits, and what documents you will have to provide to prove your eligibility for benefits. I have included examples of how earnings affect benefits. I have also included examples of how to compare options if you are eligible for two or more types of benefits.

Many people don't realize when they are paying Social Security taxes (FICA) that in addition to a Retirement Benefit, they are buying a disability insurance plan. This makes the Social Security program central to providing a "lifeline" for the disabled wage earner until he/she can return to work. You will find instructions on how to file for Disability Benefits, plus instructions on what to do if you are approved for benefits and later return to work. I have designed worksheets that will help you track your earnings and benefits to stay in compliance with Social Security rules and to avoid an overpayment.

In addition to protection for Disability Benefits, the Social Security taxes you pay earn you a survivor benefit package should you die and leave behind young children or a spouse who might qualify for Widow(er)'s Benefits. Without the survivor benefits, many young families and widow(er)s could be left with no means of financial support.

Then there is Medicare. Everything you must know to make an informed decision about Medicare can be found in this guide. Medicare is more complex than most people realize. Failure to understand the different types of Medicare benefits and enrollment periods can result in serious financial hardship. The same is true for Supplemental Medicare Insurance (Medigap). The need for this additional insurance should not be underestimated and because there is a very time-sensitive enrollment period, it is paramount you know your options.

Starting the application process can feel a bit daunting. Social Security is not only a complex program of rules and procedures, but it also has its own "language" which can be confusing. For example, two of Social Security's most frequently used terms, "eligibility," and "entitlement" have very specific meanings; "eligibility" defines the criteria to qualify for benefits; "entitlement" means you have filed an application to receive benefits. Being familiar with the terms (see Glossary) will aid you in reading this guide and in your communications with Social Security employees. Remember that Social Security employees are trained to think of themselves as public servants. They want to provide you with accurate, timely, and courteous service. I hope your experience with Social Security - be it online, by phone, or in office - will be a pleasant one.

Best Wishes,

B.J. Elgin

Social Security & Medicare Guide (Solving the Puzzle)

Table of Contents

Social Security and Medicare Contact Information

Phone
1-800-772-1213 (TTY 1-800-325-0778)
Automated Services 24 hours a day
Speak with a Representative 7:00 a.m. – 7:00 p.m. Monday through Friday
Call the 800# service to ask for your local office phone number or check your phone directory

In Office
Public Hours: 9:00 a.m. – 4:00 p.m. Monday, Tuesday, Thursday, and Friday
9:00 a.m. – 12:00 p.m. Wednesday
Check online for your local Social Security office address or call the 800# service
(To avoid a long wait at the office, make an appointment or use online services)

Online
Access Social Security's website:
www.socialsecurity.gov
Online Hours of Operation - includes holiday hours (Eastern Standard Time)
Monday – Friday – 5:00 a.m. – 1:00 a.m.
Saturday – 5:00 a.m. – 11:00 p.m.
Sunday – 8:00 a.m. – 11:30 p.m.

Use Online Services – **No need to call…….***or* **make an appointment…....***or* **go to the office.**

Apply Online for the Following Benefits
- Retirement and/or Spouse's Benefits
- Disability Benefits
- Medicare Benefits
- Extra Help (Medicare Prescription Drug Assistance)
- Supplemental Security Income (SSI) if certain requirements are met
- Appeals on some claims
  Note: At this time, applications for survivors or children cannot be filed online

It is highly recommended you file your application online. The demands on Social Security employees continue to increase. Senator Rob Portman (R-Ohio) reported in the July 21, 2014 issue of the Wall Street Journal, "Each day, 10,000 baby boomers retire and begin receiving Medicare and Social Security benefits."* Baby boomers are those born between 1946 and 1964. The last baby boomer will turn age 65 in 2029. This explains why people are waiting two to four weeks, and sometimes longer, to get an appointment; why they might be put "on hold" for 15 to 20 minutes when calling Social Security's 800# service; and/or why they are sometimes waiting for days for a return phone call from the agency.

*Portman, R. (2014, July 21). Heading Off the Entitlement Meltdown. Retrieved from https://www.wsj.com/articles/rob-portman-heading-off-the-entitlement-meltdown-1405983479

When you do an online application, the process for Social Security to pay your benefits begins on that date. If you are unsure how to answer questions, use the "Remarks" section of the online application to type your questions. After you submit your online application, it is reviewed by a Claims Specialist (CS) who will contact you to answer your questions.

In the chapters that follow, you will see a list of proofs that might be required before your application can be processed. Social Security can often access that information online and will not need proofs from you; however, if you need to submit proofs, you will be notified by Social Security. If you do not need to submit proofs, and you are already eligible for a benefit, it is possible that your first benefit could be deposited within seven to ten days from the date you file online. If there are issues that prevent your application from being processed online, you will be contacted by a Claims Specialist who can usually resolve the problem by phone.

Additionally, once you begin receiving benefits, use the online services to make changes on your record. Changes requested online are updated immediately. This ensures that any change such as a change of address or direct deposit information will not interrupt receipt of your benefits.

Issue Date for Social Security and Supplemental Security Income Benefits
Benefits are paid the month after they are due. For example, benefits due for May 2018, would have been issued (deposited) in June 2018. Social Security Benefits are issued (deposited) based on the day of the month in which you were born.
- If born between the 1st and 10th – benefits are deposited on the 2nd Wednesday
- If born between the 11th and 20th – benefits are deposited on the 3rd Wednesday
- If born between the 21st and 31st – benefits are deposited on the 4th Wednesday

Supplemental Security Income benefits are deposited on the 1st of the month. If the 1st falls on a weekend or holiday, the benefits are deposited the day before.

Create a Personal Account at www.socialsecurity.gov/myaccount
Your Social Security number unlocks a secret file of your personal information that makes you very vulnerable should it get into the hands of the wrong people. When you set up a personal account, you choose a PIN and password that will protect your Social Security records from hackers. There are many worthwhile reasons for setting up a personal account (as outlined on the next page). *You do not have to be receiving benefits*. If you do not want to use the account, you may block it. If later, you want to unblock it, you will have to contact the Social Security Administration. If you have problems setting up an online account, you can go to your local Social Security office. Take proof of your identity (i.e., U.S. driver's license, state ID card, or passport).

To Set Up your Account, you must:
- Be at least age 18
- Have a Social Security number
- Have a valid U.S. mailing address
- Have a valid email address

Be prepared to confirm some credit history information, i.e., mortgage or car loans, credit cards, etc. The reason for this is to add another level of security to your account.

With this Account, you will be able to:
- View your earnings record
- See estimates of future Social Security benefits
- Access benefit calculators to help you plan your best retirement date
- Check the status of your claim (if you have filed for benefits)
- Request a replacement Social Security card (if certain requirements are met)

If you are already receiving Social Security benefits, you may use your Personal Account to:
- Change your address and phone number
- Change the direct deposit information on your record
- Check your benefit and payment information
- Get a benefit verification letter
- Get a replacement Medicare card
- Get a Form SSA-1099 (Benefit Statement); Form 1042S for noncitizen living outside U.S.
- Report wages if you receive Disability Benefits and return to work
- Submit paystub information (if you are set up to do so)
- File a Representative Payee Accounting Report
- Check appeal status if you have an appeal pending
- Block access to your personal information

You may access the following Social Security web pages directly:

Websites of Interest:

www.socialsecurity.gov/applyonline	**Applications services**
www.socialsecurity.gov/estimator	**Estimates of future benefits**
www.socialsecurity.gov/planners	**Benefit calculators**
www.socialsecurity.gov/benefits/disability/appeal.html	**Appeal a disability claim**

Author's Website:
www.bbbenefitsguru.com
- Seminar Topics
- FAQs
- An annual update of changes in Social Security's cost of living increases, earnings test increases, and Medicare premium changes

Contacting Medicare

Phone
1-800-633-4227 (TTY 1-877-486-2048)
Automated services 24 hours a day

Online
Access Medicare's website:
www.medicare.gov

Medicare is the federal health insurance program administered by the Centers for Medicare and Medicaid Services (CMS). Once enrolled in Medicare, questions regarding health insurance benefits are to be directed to Medicare.

Enrollment in Medicare
Unless you are a Railroad retiree, you may access Social Security's online services at www.socialsecurity.gov to enroll in Medicare, change your address or request a replacement Medicare card. You may also call Social Security at 1-800-772-1213 (TTY 1-800-325-0778).

The Railroad Board (RRB) oversees all issues for railroad retirees. You may file your claim for benefits, enroll in Medicare, request replacement of a Medicare card, and make changes on your record by contacting the RRB at 1-877-772-5772 (TTY 1-312-751-4701) or access www.rrb.gov. At this time, applications for Railroad benefits must be done in-office, by phone, or by mail.

Set up your Personal Medicare Account at www.mymedicare.gov.

With this account you will be able to:
- View how much Medicare was billed for your care (often within 24-48 hours)
- View and print your list of prescriptions
- Sign up for electronic Medicare Summary Notices (MSN)
- Sign up for an electronic copy of the *Medicare and You Handbook*
- Update your list of health care providers

Other Contacts of Interest
- To report Medicare fraud, call the Office of Inspector General (OIG) 1-800-447-8477 (TTY 1-800-377-4950).
- To get help with Medicare and your secondary insurance payer problems, call the Benefits Coordinator & Recovery Center 1-855-798-2627 (TTY 1-855-797-2627).
- To locate your Agency on Aging and other agencies providing services for seniors, call the Eldercare Locator 1-800-677-1116.
- To locate your State Health Insurance Assistance Program (SHIP) representative for assistance with Medicare concerns, call 1-877-839-2675 or access their website at https://shiptacenter.org. You may also call Medicare's 800# service.

Chapter 2

Filing for Retirement Benefits

Requirements
- You must be at least age 62.
- You must have earned at least 40 credits (formerly called quarters of coverage). Credits are assigned based on your earnings. A maximum of four credits can be earned per year. The dollar amount required to earn a credit typically increases yearly. For example, in 2018 the dollar value of a credit was $1320 ($5280 = 4 credits for 2018). In 2019 the dollar value of a credit is $1360 ($5440 = 4 credits for 2019). Usually, ten years of work will result in 40 credits).
- Your earnings must be within certain limits to allow payment of benefits unless you are at or past your Full Retirement Age (FRA). See table below to determine your FRA. The earnings limit allowed is referred to as the "Earnings Test." *See Chapter 9, p. 61, "Earnings Test;" & pp. 62-64, "Earnings Test Examples."*

Full Retirement Age (FRA) Table	
Year of Birth	Age
1943-1954	66
1955	66 and 2 months
1956	66 and 4 months
1957	66 and 6 months
1958	66 and 8 months
1959	66 and 10 months
1960 and after	67
Note: Anyone born on the first day of the month is deemed to have been born the month before.	

When to Apply
You may apply as early as three months before you want your benefits to start. If you are unsure of when to apply, you may check your options by calling Social Security's 800# service or accessing Social Security's benefit planner at www.socialsecurity.gov/planners. The date you contact Social Security to schedule an appointment sets a *Protective Filing* date for you. This gives you a six-month period in which to file your application and keep the online start date or contact date as your filing date.

How to Apply (online, by phone, or in office)
- **Online** at www.socialsecurity.gov. The advantage of this is that you do not have to wait for an appointment. Due to the demand for appointments, it might be several weeks before one can be scheduled. If you do your application online but have questions, you may use the "Remarks" section of the online application to request that a Claims Specialist call you to answer your questions. See filing instructions on the next page.

Online Filing Instructions.

- o Access www.socialsecurity.gov/applyonline. You will see a screen listing the different types of benefits that can be filed online.
- o Select the application type you want to file. You will be prompted through a series of screens (similar to pages of a paper application).
- o Answer each question as instructed. If you cannot answer a question fully at that time, you may return to it later.
- o If you are inactive on a page for more than 25 minutes, you will receive a warning. You may request an extension (up to three times). You will then time out unless you resume answering questions. If you cannot complete the application in a single session, you may save it and "Return to a Saved Application" later without losing your information.
- o If you want to speak with someone at Social Security about your application, include a request in the "Remarks" section of the application for someone to call you.
- o You will receive instructions at the end of a completed application telling you what your next steps are.

- **Call** SSA at 1-800-772-1213 (TTY 1-800-325-0778). The 800# service will schedule an appointment with your local Social Security office. You can request an in-office (in-person interview) or a phone appointment.
- **Visit** your local Social Security office. To avoid a long wait, it is best to make an appointment by calling the 800# service.

Be Prepared to Answer Questions Regarding

- The date you retired or plan to retire
- An estimate of your anticipated earnings for the current year (if you are still working)
- Information on special wage payments such as sick pay, vacation pay, bonuses, etc., to be paid in the current year for work performed in a prior year
- Military service dates
- Railroad service (if five years or more)
- A pension that was not covered by Social Security taxes
- Work performed in another country that has a social security program
- Children under age 18, or under age 19 and still a full-time student in high school, or disabled before age 22. S*ee Chapter 6, pp. 26-28, "Children's Benefits."*
- Current marriage:
  - o Name of spouse (including maiden name if applicable)
  - o Social Security number (if known)
  - o Date of birth
  - o Date and city of marriage
    Note: If spouse is at least age 62, *see Chapter 3, pp. 10-14, "Spouse's Benefits."*
- Previous marriage(s):
  - o Name of spouse (including maiden name if applicable)
  - o Social Security number (if known)
  - o Date of birth
  - o Date and city of marriage
  - o Date and city of divorce and/or death (if marriage ended with death of spouse)

Note: If marriage ended in divorce, *see Chapter 4, pp. 15-19, "Divorced Spouse's Benefits."*
If marriage ended in death, *see Chapter 5, pp. 20-25, "Survivor Benefits."*
Additionally, if you are in a common-law marriage, or had a common-law marriage, contact Social Security's 800# service to ask if your state recognizes a common-law marriage.

Documents that May Be Required to Process Your Application

- Birth certificate
- Proof of citizenship or lawful alien status if not a U.S. citizen
- Military discharge (DD-214)
- W-2 form and/or self-employment tax return from previous year
- Bank information – name of financial institution, routing number, and account number (If you do not have a bank account, the benefits can be set up on a prepaid debit card. See www.GoDirect.org).
  Note: Social Security can access some proofs online and will not need those proofs from you. If you need to submit proofs, you will be notified. Social Security will copy and return proofs to you by mail.

Calculating Your Monthly Benefit Amount (MBA)

- The Primary Insurance Amount (PIA) must be calculated first (see below). The PIA would be your Monthly Benefit Amount (MBA) at your full retirement age (FRA).
- If you take the benefit before full retirement age, your PIA will be reduced 5/9 of 1% for the first 36 months and 1/12 of 1% for additional months before your full retirement age. This results in a reduced MBA. You may use the online calculators to do these calculations or you may call the Social Security Administration 800# service for assistance. *See Chapter 9, p. 56, "PIA Calculation;" & pp. 59-60, "Benefits – Age 62 vs 66 vs 70."*

Step 1
Each year of earnings is put through a formula (called indexing) to adjust the earnings to today's averages. This adjustment for inflation nets a higher benefit. Earnings beyond age 60 are not indexed.

Step 2
The highest 35 years of earnings are selected and added together. The sum is then divided by the divisor of 420 (35 years x 12 months). The result is your Average Indexed Monthly Earnings (AIME) over the 35-year period. The divisor remains the same even if you do not have 35 years of earnings on your record.

Step 3
The AIME total is put through a formula that applies set percentages to certain bend points (dollar amounts that are determined annually). The final figure is known as your Primary Insurance Amount (PIA). The PIA is your unreduced Retirement Benefit. It also determines family benefits that are payable. The actual benefit paid to you is called your Monthly Benefit Amount (MBA). *See Chapter 9, p. 56, "PIA Calculation."*

Medicare

If you are within three months of age 65 or older, *see Chapter 11, pp. 74-91, "Medicare Benefits."*

Other Factors to Consider

Delayed Retirement Credits (DRCs). You may delay taking your benefits beyond your Full Retirement Age (FRA) to earn DRCs. For each month you do not receive a benefit between your FRA and age 70, you will receive an increase of 2/3 of 1%. The Delayed Retirement Credits total 8% per year. If your FRA is 66, you could receive up to a 32% increase on your PIA at age 70. If your FRA is 67, you could receive up to a 24% increase on your PIA. The DRCs increase your Retirement Benefit for your lifetime and also increase the benefit payable to a widow(er) and/or surviving divorced spouse who might become eligible on your record. *See Chapter 9, pp. 59-60, "Benefits – Age 62 vs 66 vs 70."*

Windfall Elimination Provision (WEP). If you are eligible for a pension from another agency, i.e., the Federal Government or an employer where you did not pay Social Security taxes on your wages, your Social Security benefit could be reduced. This is called the Windfall Elimination Provision (WEP). This is a complex formula that reduces the Primary Insurance Amount (PIA) and will be calculated at the time you file your Social Security claim. You can also use the calculator at www.socialsecurity.gov/planners to figure your benefit.
Note: The WEP formula is not used for survivor benefits. *See Chapter 9, p. 57, "WEP Calculation."*

Restricted Application. If you were born before January 2, 1954 and are full retirement age, you have the option of filing for Spouse's Benefits to allow your own Retirement Benefit to earn Delayed Retirement Credits of 8% each year until age 70. The spouse on whose record you are filing must be receiving Social Security benefits unless you are filing as an Independently Entitled Divorced Spouse. *See Chapter 3, pp. 10-14, "Spouse's Benefits;" Chapter 4, pp. 15-19 "Divorced Spouse's Benefits;" & Chapter 9, pp. 67-68, "Restricted Application Calculation."*

Retirement versus Survivor benefits. If you are eligible for a Widow(er)'s or Surviving Divorced Spouse's Benefits at the time you become eligible for Retirement Benefits, explore your options. You might want to consider taking the Survivor Benefit and delaying your own Retirement Benefit until your full retirement age or until age 70 to earn Delayed Retirement Credits. *See Chapter 5, pp. 20-25, "Survivor benefits;" & Chapter 9, p. 65, "Retirement vs Survivor Benefit Calculation."*

Changes to Report (Retirement Benefits)

Important: Any of the following changes that occur after you start receiving benefits should be reported promptly. Failure to do so could cause future benefits to be delayed or could result in an overpayment that you would have to repay. You may call Social Security at 1-800-772-1213 (TTY 1-800-325-0778). If you have set up a personal account at www.socialsecurity.gov/myaccount, you may report your changes through your online account. You may also request your change by mail or visit your local Social Security office. *See Chapter 1, pp. 1-3, "Online Services."*

- If you change your address.

- If you change your Direct Deposit information.

- If you change your citizenship or immigrant status.

- If you leave the U.S. for 30 consecutive days or longer.

- If you are under full retirement age, receiving benefits and working, report any changes in the earnings estimate you provided when you filed your application.

- If you become entitled to a pension, an annuity, or sum of money for a period of employment for which you did not pay Social Security taxes.

- If you become the parent to a child (including an adopted child) who was not listed on your original application.

- If there is a stepchild receiving benefits on your record and you and the stepchild's parent divorce.

- Issues involving possible criminal behavior:

    ➢ You have an unsatisfied warrant for 30 continuous days or longer for a parole or probation violation.
    ➢ You have a warrant for your arrest for a crime or attempted crime that is a felony.
    ➢ You are confined to a jail, prison, penal institution, or correctional facility for more than 30 continuous days for conviction of a crime.
    ➢ You are confined to a public institution by court order in connection with a crime.

Chapter 3

Filing for Spouse's Benefits

Requirements
- You must be the spouse of a wage earner who has filed for benefits.
- You must be least 62 or caring for the wage earner's child(ren) under age 16 or a child who became disabled before age 22 (determined by Social Security) and requires a level of care called personal services (assistance with feeding, bathing, and dressing).
- You cannot be eligible for a Social Security benefit on your own work record that is more than 50% of what your unreduced Spouse's Benefit would be. *If born before January 2, 1954, see Chapter 9, pp. 67-68, "Restricted Application Calculation."*
- Your earnings must be within certain limits to allow payment of benefits unless you are at or past your Full Retirement Age (FRA). See table below to determine your FRA. The earnings limit allowed is referred to as the "Earnings Test." *See Chapter 9, p. 61, "Earnings Test;" & pp. 62-64, "Earnings Test Examples."*

Full Retirement Age (FRA) Table	
Year of Birth	Age
1943-1954	66
1955	66 and 2 months
1956	66 and 4 months
1957	66 and 6 months
1958	66 and 8 months
1959	66 and 10 months
1960 and after	67
Note: Anyone born on the first day of the month is deemed to have been born the month before.	

When to Apply
File three months before you want your benefits to start. If you are unsure of when to apply, you may check your options by calling Social Security's 800# service or accessing Social Security's benefit planner at www.socialsecurity.gov/planners. The date you contact Social Security to schedule an appointment sets a *Protective Filing* date for you. This gives you a six-month period in which to file your application and keep the online start date or contact date as your filing date.

How to Apply (online, by phone, or in office)
- **Online** at www.socialsecurity.gov. The advantage of this is that you do not have to wait for an appointment. Due to the demand for appointments, it might be several weeks before one can be scheduled. If you do your application online but have questions, you may use the "Remarks" section of the online application to request that a Claims Specialist call you to answer your questions. See filing instructions below.
    #### Online Filing Instructions
    - Access www.socialsecurity.gov/applyonline. You will see a screen listing the different types of applications that can be filed online.

- o Select the "Retirement Benefit" option, then select the option to file for Spouse's Benefits. You will be prompted through a series of screens (similar to pages of a paper application).
  - o Answer each question as instructed. If you cannot answer a question fully at that time, you may return to it later.
  - o If you are inactive on a page for more than 25 minutes, you will receive a warning. You may request an extension (up to three times). You will then time out unless you resume answering questions. If you cannot complete the application in a single session, you may save it and "Return to a Saved Application" later without losing your information.
  - o Type "I want Spouse's Benefits" in the Remarks section of the application. If you want to speak with someone at Social Security about your application, also include a request in the "Remarks" section for someone to call you.
  - o You will receive instructions at the end of your completed application telling you what your next steps are.
- **Call** SSA at 1-800-772-1213 (TTY 1-800-325-0778). The 800# service will schedule an appointment with your local Social Security field office. You can request an in-office (in-person interview) or a phone appointment.
- **Visit** your local Social Security Administration office. To avoid a long wait, it is best to schedule an appointment.

Be Prepared to Answer Questions Regarding
- The wage earner's name and Social Security number
- Military service dates
- Railroad service (if five years or more)
- An estimate of your anticipated earnings for the current year (if you are still working)
- Pension that was not covered by Social Security taxes
- Work performed in another country that has a social security program
- Children under age 18, under age 19 and still a full-time student in high school or disabled before age 22. *See Chapter 6, pp. 26-28, "Children's Benefits."*
- Current marriage:
  - o Name of spouse (including maiden name if applicable)
  - o Social Security number (if known)
  - o Date of birth
  - o Date and city of marriage
- Previous marriage(s):
  - o Name of spouse (including maiden name if applicable)
  - o Social Security number (if known)
  - o Date of birth
  - o Date and city of marriage
  - o Date and city of divorce and/or death (if marriage ended with death of spouse)
    Note: If marriage ended in divorce, *see Chapter 4, pp. 15-19, "Divorced Spouse's Benefits,"* If marriage ended in death, *see Chapter 5, pp. 20-25, "Survivor Benefits."*
    Additionally, if you are in a common-law marriage or had a common-law marriage, contact Social Security's 800# service to ask if your state recognizes common-law marriage.

Documents that May be Required to Process your Application

- Birth Certificate
- Proof of Citizenship or lawful alien status if not a U.S. citizen
- Proof of marriage
- If working, W-2 form from previous year or if self-employed, your self-employment tax return from prior year
- Bank information – name of financial institution, routing number, and account number
  If you do not have a bank account, you may request your benefits be issued by a prepaid debit card. See www.GoDirect.org.
- If under age 62 and you are the parent to children as defined above, *see Chapter 6, pp. 26-28, "Children's Benefits."*
  Note: Social Security can access some proofs online and will not need those proofs from you. If you need to submit proofs, you will be notified. Social Security will copy and return them to you.

Calculating Your Monthly Benefit Amount (MBA)

The unreduced benefit amount, called the Primary Insurance Amount (PIA), must be calculated for the wage earner on whose record benefits will be paid.

Step 1
Each year of earnings is put through a formula (called indexing) to adjust the earnings to today's averages. This adjustment for inflation nets a higher benefit.

Step 2
The highest 35 years of earnings are selected and added together. The sum is then divided by the divisor of 420 (35 years x 12 months). The result is the Average Indexed Monthly Earnings (AIME) over the 35-year period. The divisor remains the same even if the wage earner does not have 35 years of earnings on record. If the benefits being paid are on the record of a disabled wage earner, the number of years (and divisor) used to compute the PIA will vary. *See Chapter 8, p. 37, "Disability Benefits."*

Step 3
The AIME total is put through a formula that applies set percentages to certain bend points (dollar amounts that are determined annually). The final figure is known as the Primary Insurance Amount (PIA). The PIA is the unreduced Retirement Benefit. It also determines family benefits that are payable. The actual benefit paid to you is called your Monthly Benefit Amount (MBA). *See Chapter 9, p. 56, "PIA Calculation."*

The Spouse's Benefit is never more than 50% of the wage earner's Primary Insurance Amount (PIA). There are several factors that must be considered to determine how much the spouse will receive.

- If the Spouse's Benefit is started before his/her full retirement age, the 50% amount is reduced 25/36 of 1% per month for the first 36 months before full retirement age and 5/12 of 1% for any additional months before full retirement age. If there are eligible children under age 16 in the spouse's care, the Spouse's Benefit is not reduced for age.
- If the spouse is eligible for benefits on his/her own Social Security record, that benefit must be calculated first and then the difference due as a spouse is calculated and added to it. Different reduction factors (percentages) apply for a Retirement Benefit versus a

Spouse's Benefit, making it necessary to calculate them separately. *See Chapter 9, p. 66, "Spouse and Divorced Spouse Benefit Calculation."*

- If there are children eligible on the record, the Family Maximum must be considered. The Family Maximum is usually between 150% to 180% of the wage earner's PIA. The Family Maximum limits the amount of benefits that can be paid to beneficiaries. *See Chapter 9, p. 69, "Child's Benefit Calculation;" & p. 70, "Family Maximum."*

Medicare

If you are within three months of age 65 or older, *see Chapter 11, pp. 74-91, "Medicare."*

Other Factors to Consider

Government Pension Offset (GPO). If you receive a pension from an employer, such as a federal, state, or county government agency, and you did not pay Social Security taxes to earn that pension, you will have an offset against Social Security benefits payable to you as a spouse, ex-spouse, or survivor. The offset is as follows: Compare 2/3 of the non-social security pension to what is payable from Social Security.

> **Example**: Cindy has a Civil Service pension of $1500 per month. She is due a Social Security Spouse's Benefit of $1200 per month. Because 2/3 of her Civil Service pension is $1000, Cindy would be due only $200 per month in Spouse's Benefits. You may also use the online calculator at **www.socialsecurity.gov/planners**.

> *Note:* *If the other pension is taken as a lump sum payment, Social Security will apply the offset by calculating what the monthly pension would be as if it had been set up monthly.*

Restricted Application. If you were born before January 2, 1954 and are full retirement age, you have the option of filing for Spouse's Benefits and delaying your own Retirement Benefit until age 70. This would allow your Retirement Benefit to increase by 2/3 of 1% (8% yearly) for each month you do not receive your Retirement Benefit before age 70. The spouse on whose record you are filing must be receiving Social Security benefits. *See Chapter 9, pp. 67-68, "Restricted Application Calculation."*

Changes to Report (Spouse's Benefits)

Important: Any of the following changes that occur after you start receiving benefits should be reported promptly. Failure to do so could cause future benefits to be delayed or could result in an overpayment that you would have to repay. You may call Social Security at 1-800-772-1213 (TTY 1-800-325-0778) or, if you have set up a personal account at www.socialsecurity.gov/myaccount, you may report most of your changes through your online account. You may also request your change by mail or visit your local Social Security office. *See Chapter 1, pp. 1-3, "Online Services."*

- If you change your address.

- If you change your Direct Deposit information.

- If you change your citizenship or immigrant status.

- If you leave the U.S. for 30 consecutive days or longer.

- If you change your marital status – marriage, divorce or annulment.

- If a Social Security beneficiary in your care or custody leaves your care or dies.

- If you are under full retirement age, receiving benefits and working, report any changes in the earnings estimate you provided when you filed your application.

- If you become entitled to a pension, an annuity, or sum of money for a period of employment for which you did not pay Social Security taxes.

- If you become the parent to a child (including an adopted child) who was not listed on your original application.

- If there is a stepchild receiving benefits on your record and you and the stepchild's parent divorce.

- Issues involving possible criminal behavior:

  ➢ You have an unsatisfied warrant for 30 continuous days or longer for a parole or probation violation.
  ➢ You have a warrant for your arrest for a crime or attempted crime that is a felony.
  ➢ You are confined to a jail, prison, penal institution or correctional facility for more than 30 continuous days for conviction of a crime.
  ➢ You are confined to a public institution by court order in connection with a crime.

Chapter 4

Filing for Divorced Spouse's Benefits

Requirements:

- You must be at least age 62.
- Your marriage must have lasted at least ten years.
- You are not currently married.
- You cannot be eligible for a Social Security benefit on your own work record that is more than 50% of what your unreduced Divorced Spouse's Benefit would be. *If born before January 2, 1954, see Chapter 9, pp. 67-68, "Restricted Application Calculation."*
- Ex-spouse on whom you are filing has filed for his/her own Social Security benefits. *Exception*: An Independently Entitled Divorced Spouse is eligible even if the ex-spouse has not filed for his/her own benefits. All criteria above must be met, and the divorce has to have occurred at least two years earlier.
- Your earnings must be within certain limits to allow payment of benefits unless you are at or past your Full Retirement Age (FRA). See table below to determine your FRA. The earnings limit allowed is referred to as the "Earnings Test." *See Chapter 9, p. 61, "Earnings Test;" & pp. 62-64, "Earnings Test Examples."*

Full Retirement Age (FRA) Table	
Year of Birth	Age
1943-1954	66
1955	66 and 2 months
1956	66 and 4 months
1957	66 and 6 months
1958	66 and 8 months
1959	66 and 10 months
1960 and after	67
Note: Anyone born on the first day of the month is deemed to have been born the month before.	

When to Apply

File three months before you want your benefits to start. If you are unsure of when to apply, you may check your options by calling Social Security's 800# service or accessing Social Security's benefit planner at www.socialsecurity.gov/planners. The date you contact Social Security to schedule an appointment sets a *Protective Filing* date for you. This gives you a six-month period in which to file your application and keep the online start date or contact date as your filing date.

How to Apply (online, by phone, or in office)

- **Online** at www.socialsecurity.gov. The advantage of this is that you do not have to wait for an appointment. Due to the demand for appointments, it might be several weeks before one can be scheduled. If you do your application online, you may use the "Remarks" section of the online application to request that a Claims Specialist call you to answer any questions you might have. See filing instructions on the next page.

Online Filing Instructions.

- ○ Access www.socialsecurity.gov/applyonline. You will see a screen listing the different types of applications that can be filed online.
- ○ Select the "Retirement Benefits" option, then select the option to file for Spouse's Benefits. You will be prompted through a series of screens (similar to pages of a paper application).
- ○ Answer each question as instructed. If you cannot answer a question fully at that time, you may return to it later.
- ○ If you are inactive on a page for more than 25 minutes, you will receive a warning. You may request an extension (up to three times). You will then time out unless you resume answering questions. If you cannot complete the application in a single session, you may save it and "Return to a Saved Application" later without losing your information.
- ○ In the "Remarks" section, type, "I am filing for Divorced Spouse's Benefits." If you want to speak with someone at Social Security about your application, also include a request in this section for someone to call you.
- ○ You will receive instructions at the end of a completed application telling you what your next steps are.
- **Call** SSA at 1-800-772-1213 (TTY 1-800-325-0778). The 800# service will schedule an appointment with your local Social Security office. You can request an in-office (in-person interview) or a phone appointment.
- **Visit** your local Social Security office. To avoid a long wait, it is best to schedule an appointment.

Be Prepared to Answer Questions Regarding

- The wage earner's name and Social Security number
- Military service dates
- Railroad service (if five years or more)
- An estimate of your anticipated earnings for the current year (if you are still working)
- If you are eligible for a pension that was not covered by Social Security taxes
- Work performed in another country that has a social security program
- Details on Previous marriage(s):
  - ○ Name of spouse (including maiden name if applicable)
  - ○ Social Security number (if known)
  - ○ Date of birth
  - ○ Date and city of marriage
  - ○ Date and city of divorce
    Note: *If divorced spouse is deceased, see Chapter 5, pp. 20-25, "Survivor benefits." Additionally, if you are in a common-law marriage or had a common-law marriage, contact Social Security's 800# service to ask if your state recognizes a common-law marriage.*

Documents That May be Required to Process your Application

- Birth certificate
- If not U.S. born, proof of citizenship or lawful alien status
- Proof of marriage

- Proof of divorce
- If working, W-2 form from previous year, or if self-employed, your self-employment tax return from prior year
- Bank information: name of financial institution, routing number, and account number
  If no bank account, you may request your benefits be issued by a prepaid debit card, see www.GoDirect.org.
  Note: Social Security can access some proofs online and will not need those proofs from you. If you need to submit proofs, you will be notified. Social Security will copy and return them to you.

Calculating your Monthly Benefit Amount (MBA)

The unreduced benefit amount, called the Primary Insurance Amount (PIA), must be calculated for the wage earner on whose record benefits will be paid.

Step 1

Each year of earnings is put through a formula (called indexing) to adjust the earnings to today's averages. This adjustment for inflation nets a higher benefit.

Step 2

The highest 35 years of earnings are selected and added together. The sum is then divided by the divisor of 420 (35 years x 12 months). The result is the Average Indexed Monthly Earnings (AIME) over the 35-year period. The divisor remains the same even if the wage earner does not have 35 years of earnings on your record. If the benefits being paid are on the record of a disabled wage earner, the number of years (and divisor) used to compute the PIA will vary. *See Chapter 8, p. 37, "Disability Benefits."*

Step 3

The AIME total is put through a formula that applies set percentages to certain bend points (dollar amounts that are determined annually). The final figure is known as the Primary Insurance Amount (PIA). The PIA is the unreduced Retirement Benefit. It also determines family benefits that are payable. The actual benefit paid to you is called your Monthly Benefit Amount (MBA). *See Chapter 9, p. 56, "PIA Calculation."*

The Divorced Spouse's Benefit is never more than 50% of the wage earner's full Primary Insurance Amount (PIA). A Divorced Spouse's Benefit does not affect benefits paid to a current spouse or children. The following factors must be considered to determine how much the divorced spouse will receive:

- The age at which the Divorced Spouse's Benefit begins. If the Divorced Spouse's Benefit is started before his/her full retirement age, the 50% amount is reduced 25/36 of 1% for the first 36 months before full retirement age and 5/12 of 1% for any additional months before full retirement age.
- If the divorced spouse is eligible for benefits on his/her own Social Security record, that benefit must be calculated first and the difference due as a divorced spouse is added to it. Different reduction percentages apply for a Retirement Benefit versus a Spouse's Benefit making it necessary to calculate them separately. *See Chapter 9, p. 66, "Spouse and Divorced Spouse Benefit Calculation;" & pp. 67-68, "Restricted Application."*

Medicare

If you are within three months of age 65 or older, *see Chapter 11, pp. 74-91, "Medicare."*

Other Factors to Consider

Government Pension Offset (GPO). If you receive a pension from an employer, such as a federal, state, or county government agency, and you did not pay Social Security taxes to earn that pension, you will have an offset against Social Security benefits payable to you as a spouse, ex-spouse, or survivor. The offset is as follows: Compare 2/3 of the non-social security pension to what is payable from Social Security.

> **Example:** Cindy has a Civil Service pension of $1500 per month. She is due a Divorced Spouse's Benefit of $1200 per month. Because 2/3 of her Civil Service pension is $1000, Cindy would be due only $200 per month in Divorced Spouse's Benefits. You may also use the online calculator at www.socialsecurity.gov/plannners.
>
> *Note: If the other pension is taken as a lump sum payment, Social Security will apply the offset by calculating what the monthly pension would be as if it had been set up monthly.*

Restricted Application. If you were born before January 2, 1954 and are full retirement age, you have the option of filing for Divorced Spouse's Benefits and delaying your own Retirement Benefit until age 70. This would allow your Retirement Benefit to increase by 2/3 of 1% (8% yearly) for each month you do not receive your Retirement Benefit before age 70. The spouse on whose record you are filing must be receiving Social Security benefits unless you are filing as an Independently Entitled Divorced Spouse. *See Chapter 9, pp. 67-68, "Restricted Application Calculation."*

Changes to Report (Divorced Spouse's Benefits)

Important: Any of the following changes that occur after you start receiving benefits should be reported promptly. Failure to do so could cause future benefits to be delayed or could result in an overpayment that you would have to repay. You may call Social Security at 1-800-772-1213 (TTY 1-800-325-0778) or, if you have set up a personal account at www.socialsecurity.gov/myaccount, you may report most of your changes through your online account. You may also request your change by mail or visit your local Social Security office. *See Chapter 1, pp. 1-3, "Online Services."*

- If you change your address.

- If you change your Direct Deposit information.

- If you change your citizenship or immigrant status.

- If you leave the U.S. for 30 consecutive days or longer.

- If you change your marital status – marriage, divorce or annulment.

- If a Social Security beneficiary in your care or custody leaves your care or dies.

- If you are under full retirement age, receiving benefits and working, report any changes in the earnings estimate you provided when you filed your application.

- If you become entitled to a pension, an annuity, or sum of money for a period of employment for which you did not pay Social Security taxes.

- If you become the parent to a child (including an adopted child) who was not listed on your original application.

- If there is a stepchild receiving benefits on your record and you and the stepchild's parent divorce.

- Issues involving possible criminal behavior:

  - You have an unsatisfied warrant for 30 continuous days or longer for a parole or probation violation.
  - You have a warrant for your arrest for a crime or attempted crime that is a felony.
  - You are confined to a jail, prison, penal institution or correctional facility for more than 30 continuous days for conviction of a crime.
  - You are confined to a public institution by court order in connection with a crime.

Filing for Survivor Benefits

Requirements

The deceased person (wage earner) must have sufficient Social Security credits. Usually, ten years of work are required. There are exceptions for younger wage earners. Contact Social Security for more information regarding these exceptions.

Types of Survivor Benefits

Lump Sum Death Benefit. A one-time $255 payment that is paid to the spouse who was living with the deceased. If the spouse was not living with the deceased, then he/she must be eligible for a Widow(er)'s Benefit. If there is no eligible spouse, it can be paid to eligible child(ren).

Widow(er)'s Benefits.

- You must be at least age 60
- You must be at least age 50 for Disabled Widow(er)'s Benefits (DWB). Disability must be established at the time of the wage earner's death or within seven years following the wage earner's death. *See Chapter 8, pp. 34-55, "Disability Benefits."*
- You must have been married for at least nine months preceding the month of wage earner's death. Some exceptions apply to the nine-month rule if death was accidental.
- You must not be currently married, unless remarried after age 60, or age 50 for DWB.
- If receiving benefits on your own record or on another Social Security record, a comparison should be done by Social Security to determine what benefit will be more advantageous.
- Your earnings must be within certain limits to allow payment of benefits unless you are at or past your Full Retirement Age (FRA). See table below to determine your FRA. The earnings limits allowed are referred to as the "Earnings Test." *See Chapter 9, p. 61, "Earnings Test;" & pp. 62-64, "Earnings Test Examples."*

Full Retirement Age (FRA) Table for Widow(er)'s Benefits	
Date of Birth	**Age**
Before 1/1/40	65
1/2/40 to 1/1/41	65 and 2 months
1/2/41 to 1/1/42	65 and 4 months
1/2/42 to 1/1/43	65 and 6 months
1/2/43 to 1/1/44	65 and 8 months
1/2/44 to 1/1/45	65 and 10 months
1/2/45 to 1/1/57	66
1/2/57 to 1/1/58	66 and 2 months
1/2/58 to 1/1/59	66 and 4 months
1/2/59 to 1/1/60	66 and 6 months
1/2/60 to 1/1/61	66 and 8 months
1/2/61 to 1/1/62	66 and 10 months
1/2/62 or later	67
Note: Anyone born on the first day of the month is deemed to have been born the month before.	

Surviving Divorced Spouse's Benefits.
- You must be at least age 60, or
- You must be at least age 50 for Disabled Surviving Divorced Spouse's Benefits and be disabled at the time of the wage earner's death or within seven years following the wage earner's death. *See Chapter 8, pp. 34-55, "Disability Benefits."*
- You must have been married to the deceased wage earner at least 10 years.
- If remarried, marriage must have occurred after age 60 or age 50 if filing as a Disabled Surviving Divorced Spouse.
- If receiving benefits on your own record or a benefit on another Social Security record, that benefit cannot exceed the survivor benefit.
- Your earnings must be within certain limits to allow payment of benefits unless you are at or past your Full Retirement Age (FRA). See table on previous page to determine your full retirement age. The earnings limits allowed are referred to as the "Earnings Test." *See Chapter 9, p. 61, "Earnings Test;" & pp. 62-64, "Earnings Test Examples."*

Mother's/Father's Benefits. Benefit is payable to a mother/father who is caring for an eligible child of the deceased. Child must be under age 16 or disabled before age 22 and requiring personal services (assistance with feeding, bathing, and dressing). If mother/father is working, earnings must meet certain limitations. *See Chapter 9, p. 61, "Earnings Test;" & pp. 62-64, "Earnings Test Examples."*

Children's Benefits. Benefits are payable to the eligible child, stepchild, or adopted child of the deceased wage earner. Child must be under age 18, or age 19 if a full-time student in high school, or disabled before age 22. If child is working, earnings cannot exceed the allowable limit. *See Chapter 6, pp. 26-28, "Children's Benefit;" & Chapter 9, p. 61, "Earnings Test;" & pp. 62-64, "Earnings Test Examples."*

Grandchildren's Benefits. Grandchildren under age 18, or age 19 if a full-time student in high school, or disabled before age 22, can qualify on the record of a grandparent if both parents of the child(ren) are either deceased or disabled at the time the grandparent becomes eligible for benefits or dies. If a grandchild is working, his/her earnings cannot exceed the allowable limit. *See Chapter 6, pp. 26-28, "Children's Benefits;" & Chapter 9, p. 61, "Earnings Test;" & pp. 62-64, "Earnings Test Examples."*

Parent's Benefits. A parent who was a dependent of a deceased wage earner who had earned credits for Social Security benefits might be eligible for benefits on that child's Social Security record. The parent must be at least age 62 and must have been receiving at least one-half support from his/her deceased child at the time of child's death (or at the start of the deceased child's disability). The parent's own Social Security benefit cannot exceed what the Parent Benefit would be. A parent must provide proof that the deceased wage earner (child) was providing at least one-half of the parent's support. If the parent is working, earnings cannot exceed the allowable limit. *See Chapter 9, p. 61, "Earnings Test;" & pp. 62-64, "Earnings Test Examples."*

When to Apply

Contact the Social Security Administration upon the death of a wage earner who would make you eligible for any of the benefits listed above. The date you contact Social Security to schedule an appointment sets a *Protective Filing* date for you. This gives you a six-month period in which to file your application and keep the contact date as your filing date.

Note: If you qualify as a widow or surviving divorced spouse and are already receiving Spouse's or Divorced Spouse's Benefits on the wage earner's record at the time of his/her death, and you are not full retirement age (see Chart on page 20), you will need to complete a *Form SSA-4111* agreeing to accept a reduced survivor benefit. You may retrieve the form online at www.socialsecurity.gov, complete it, sign it, and mail it or take it to your local Social Security office. Do this timely to avoid interruption of your benefit.

How to Apply (by phone or in office)

- **Call** SSA at 1-800-772-1213 (TTY 1-800-325-0778). The 800# service will schedule an appointment with your local Social Security office. You can request an in-office appointment (in-person interview) or a phone appointment.
- **Visit** your local Social Security office. To avoid a long wait, it is best to schedule an appointment.
  Note: At this time, applications for survivor benefits cannot be filed online.

Be Prepared to Answer Questions Regarding

- The deceased wage earner's Social Security number
- Date and place of birth
- Date and place of death for the wage earner
- Military service for the deceased wage earner and yourself
- Railroad service (if more than five years) for the deceased wage earner and yourself
- Current and previous year of earnings for the deceased wage earner and yourself
- Pensions not covered by Social Security taxes for deceased wage earner and yourself
- Work performed in another country that has a social security program for deceased wage earner and yourself
- Children under age 18, or under age 19 and still a full-time student in high school, or disabled before age 22. *See Chapter 6, pp. 26-28, "Children's Benefits."*
- Marriage information for the deceased wage earner and yourself
  Current marriage:
  - o Name of spouse (including maiden name if applicable)
  - o Social Security number (if known)
  - o Date and place of birth
  - o Date and place of marriage
  Previous marriage(s):
  - o Name of spouse (including maiden name if applicable)
  - o Social Security number (if known)
  - o Date and place of birth
  - o Date and place of marriage
  - o Date and place of divorce, and/or death if previous marriage ended in death
    Note: If marriage ended in divorce, *see Chapter 4, pp. 15-19, "Divorced Spouse's Benefit." Additionally, if you are in a common-law marriage, or had a common-law marriage, contact Social Security's 800# service to ask if your state recognizes a common-law marriage.*

Documents That May be Required to Process your Application

- Proof of wage earner's death
- Your birth certificate
- Your marriage certificate

- Military Service Discharge (DD-214) for the deceased
- Your divorce papers, if filing as a divorced spouse
- Birth certificates and Social Security numbers for eligible children
- Deceased wage earner's W-2 forms or self-employment tax returns for current and prior year if applicable
- Bank information: name of financial institution, routing number, and account number
  If no bank account, you may request your benefits to be issued by a prepaid debit card. See www.GoDirect.org.
  Note: Social Security can access some proofs online and will not need those proofs from you. If you need to submit proofs, you will be notified. Social Security will copy and return them to you by mail.

Calculating your Monthly Benefit Amount (MBA)

The unreduced benefit amount, called the Primary Insurance Amount (PIA), must be calculated for the wage earner on whose record benefits will be paid.

Step 1
Each year of earnings is put through a formula (called indexing) to adjust the earnings to today's averages. This adjustment nets a higher benefit.

Step 2
Generally, the highest 35 years of earnings are selected and added together. The sum is then divided by the divisor of 420 (35 years x 12 months). The result is the Average Indexed Monthly Earnings (AIME) over the 35-year period. If the wage earner dies before retirement age, the number of years used to compute the AIME will vary depending on the age of death. Generally, the years used in the computation begin with age 22 and end with the year of death. The divisor is then 12 x the number of years to be used in the computation.

Step 3
The AIME total is put through a formula that applies set percentages to certain bend points (dollar amounts that are determined annually). The final figure is known as the Primary Insurance Amount (PIA). This is the amount used to determine benefits paid to survivors on the record. The actual benefit paid to you is called your Monthly Benefit Amount (MBA). *See Chapter 9, p. 56, "PIA Calculation."*

Calculating Survivor benefits can be very complex. Social Security employees rely on software programs designed to calculate the Widow(er)'s and/or Surviving Divorced Spouse's Benefit based on several factors.

- A widow(er) or surviving divorced spouse, at full retirement age, will be eligible for 100% of the deceased wage earner's PIA if the deceased had never received reduced benefits. The benefit amount could also be increased if the deceased was or would have been eligible for Delayed Retirement Credits at the time of his/her death.
- If the deceased received reduced benefits, Social Security will determine what formula will be used to calculate the Widow(er)'s or Surviving Divorced Spouse's Benefit.
- If the widow(er) or surviving divorced spouse is electing benefits before full retirement age, the widow(er)'s reduction factor must also be considered. This can range from 19/40 of 1% to 19/56 of 1% per month depending on his/her year of birth.
- If the widow(er) or surviving divorced spouse is receiving his/her own Retirement Benefit and the survivor benefit is higher, only the difference is paid.

- If multiple survivors are due benefits on the record, the Family Maximum payable must be considered. It is between 150% to 180% of the Primary Insurance Amount (PIA). A Surviving Divorced Spouse's Benefit does not affect the Family Maximum for other survivors due on the record. *See Chapter 9, p. 70, "Family Maximum Calculation."*

Medicare
If you are within three months of age 65 or older, *See Chapter 11, pp. 74-91, "Medicare."*

Other Factors to Consider
Retirement versus Survivor benefits.
If you become eligible for more than one type of Social Security benefit and you are not yet age 70, you should consider your options. This situation often arises if you become eligible for retirement and survivor benefits simultaneously.

Calculate what the different benefit amounts would be for a Widow(er) or Surviving Divorced Spouse's Benefit versus your Retirement Benefit. Also, consider the different ages you could start the benefits. Determine if Delayed Retirement Credits could increase one of the benefits. If so, that might be the benefit you want to delay taking until you are age 70. Once you know the differences in the amounts, you can calculate what is most advantageous for you. There are calculators on Social Security's website to help you with this or you may call the 800# service to ask for assistance or make an appointment to talk with a Social Security Claims Specialist. Do not be reluctant to ask for assistance. Because of the complex calculations involved, this process can be very confusing and frustrating.

A Claims Specialist can help you calculate the different options, but he/she cannot advise you what to do. You must make that decision based on the information provided you. *See Chapter 9, pp. 59-60, "Benefits – Age 62 vs Age 66 vs Age 70 Calculations;" & p. 65, "Retirement vs Survivor Benefits Calculation."*

Government Pension Offset (GPO).
If you receive a pension from an employer, such as a federal, state, or county government agency, and you did not pay Social Security taxes to earn that pension, you will have an offset against Social Security benefits payable to you as a spouse, ex-spouse, or survivor. The offset is as follows: Compare 2/3 of the non-social security pension to what is payable from Social Security.

Example: Cindy has a Civil Service pension of $1500 per month. She is due a SS Spouse's Benefit of $1200 per month. Because 2/3 of her Civil Service pension is $1000, Cindy would be due only $200 per month in Spouse's Benefits. You may also use the online calculator at www.socialsecurity.gov/planners.

Note: If the other pension is taken as a lump sum payment, Social Security will apply the offset by calculating what the monthly pension would be as if it had been set up monthly.

Changes to Report (Survivor Benefits)

Important: Any of the following changes that occur after you start receiving benefits should be reported promptly. Failure to do so could cause future benefits to be delayed or could result in an overpayment that you would have to repay. You may call Social Security at 1-800-772-1213 (TTY 1-800-325-0778) or, if you have set up a personal account at www.socialsecurity.gov/myaccount, you may report most of your changes through your online account. You may also request your change by mail or visit your local Social Security office. *See Chapter 1, pp. 1-3, "Online Services."*

- If you change your address.

- If you change your Direct Deposit information.

- If you change your citizenship or immigrant status.

- If you leave the U.S. for 30 consecutive days or longer.

- If you change your marital status – marriage, divorce or annulment.

- If a Social Security beneficiary in your care or custody leaves your care or dies.

- If you are under full retirement age and receiving benefits and working, report any changes in the earnings estimate you provided when you filed your application.

- If you become entitled to a pension, an annuity, or sum of money for a period of employment for which you did not pay Social Security taxes.

- If you become the parent to a child (including an adopted child) who was not listed on your original application.

- If there is a stepchild receiving benefits on your record and you and the stepchild's parent divorce.

- Issues involving possible criminal behavior:

  - You have an unsatisfied warrant for 30 continuous days or longer for a parole or probation violation.
  - You have a warrant for your arrest for a crime or attempted crime that is a felony.
  - You are confined to a jail, prison, penal institution or correctional facility for more than 30 continuous days for conviction of a crime.
  - You are confined to a public institution by court order in connection with a crime.

Filing for Children's Benefits
(Natural, Adopted, Stepchildren, and/or Grandchildren)

Requirements
- Child(ren) must be unmarried and eligible on the record of a wage earner who is filing for, or receiving Retirement or Disability Benefits, or is deceased and has enough credits for survivor benefits to be payable.
- Child(ren) must be the natural, legally adopted, or dependent stepchild.
- If filing for a grandchild, both parents of the child must be deceased or disabled at the time the grandparent becomes eligible for his/her own benefits or the grandparent dies.
- Child(ren) must be under age 18, or age 19 if a full-time student in high school, or disabled before age 22.
- Child's earnings must be within certain limits to allow payment. The earnings limits allowed are referred to as the "Earnings Test." *See Chapter 9, p. 61, "Earnings Test;" & pp. 62-64, "Earnings Test Examples."*

When to Apply
Contact the Social Security Administration when a child (as defined above) becomes eligible for benefits based on a wage earner's retirement, survivor, or disability record. The date you contact Social Security to schedule an appointment sets a *Protective Filing* date for the children. This gives you a six-month period in which to file your application and keep the contact date as the filing date.

How to Apply (by phone or in office)
- **Call** SSA at 1-800-772-1213 (TTY 1-800-325-0778). The 800# service will schedule an appointment with your local Social Security office. You can request an in-office appointment (in-person interview) or a phone appointment.
- **Visit** your local Social Security office. To avoid a long wait, it is best to schedule an appointment.
  Note: ***At this time, applications for Children's Benefits cannot be filed online.***

Be Prepared to Answer Questions Regarding
- Name and Social Security number of wage earner on whose record you are filing
- Military service dates for the wage earner
- Railroad service (if five years or more) for the wage earner
- Earnings information for the wage earner
- Work performed by the wage earner in another country that has a social security program
- Name, Social Security number, and date of birth for child(ren)
- If child is between age 18-19, information on full-time school attendance
- If child is over age 18 but was considered to be 100% disabled before age 22, provide information regarding child's disability *See Chapter 8, pp. 34-55, "Disability Benefits."*
- If child is working, need an estimate of expected earnings for the current and future year

Documents That May be Required to Process Your Application
- Birth certificate(s) for child(ren)
- Adoption decree(s) for adopted child(ren)
- Marriage certificate of parents if filing for stepchild(ren)
- Proof of citizenship or lawful alien status if not a U.S. citizen
- Proof of death or disability of child(ren)'s parents if filing for a grandchild(ren)
- Bank information: name of financial institution, routing number, and account number
  If no bank account, you may request that your benefits be issued by a prepaid debit card.
  See www.GoDirect.org.
  Note: Social Security can access some proofs online and will not need those proofs from you. If you need to submit proofs, you will be notified. Social Security will copy and return them to you.

Calculating the Monthly Benefit Amount (MBA) for Child(ren)
The unreduced benefit amount, called the Primary Insurance Amount (PIA), must be calculated for the wage earner on whose record benefits will be paid.

Step 1
Each year of earnings is put through a formula (called indexing) to adjust the earnings to today's averages. This adjustment for inflation nets a higher benefit.

Step 2
On a retirement record, the highest 35 years of earnings are selected and added together. The sum is then divided by the divisor of 420 (35 years x 12 months). The result is the Average Indexed Monthly Earnings (AIME) over the 35-year period. The divisor remains the same even if the wage earner does not have 35 years of earnings except for younger wage earners. **Note: If the wage earner becomes disabled or dies before age 62, there are fewer years used in the computation of the AIME.** Generally, the years used in the computation begin with age 22 and end with the year the disability began or with the year of death. The divisor is then 12 x the number of years to be used in the computation.

Step 3
The AIME total is put through a formula that applies set percentages to certain bend points (dollar amounts that are determined annually). The final figure is known as the Primary Insurance Amount (PIA). This is the amount used to determine benefits that can be paid to a child(ren) on the record. The actual benefit paid is called the Monthly Benefit Amount (MBA). *See Chapter 9, p.56, "PIA Calculation."*

- A child is due up to 50% of the Primary Insurance Amount on the Social Security record of a retired or disabled parent, qualifying stepparent or grandparent.
- A child is due up to 75% of the Primary Insurance Amount on the Social Security record of a deceased parent, qualifying stepparent or grandparent.
  Note: The Family Maximum must be considered if two or more beneficiaries (other than the wage earner) are being paid on the record. *See Chapter 9, p. 69, "Child's Benefit Calculation;" & p. 70, "Family Maximum Calculation."*

Changes to Report (Children's Social Security Benefits)

Important: Any of the following changes that occur after you start receiving benefits for a child should be reported promptly. Failure to do so could cause future benefits to be delayed or could result in an overpayment that you would have to repay. You may call Social Security at 1-800-772-1213 (TTY 1-800-325-0778) or you may report most of your changes through your online account at www.socialsecurity.gov/myaccount. You may also request your change by mail or visit your local Social Security office. *See Chapter 1, pp. 1-3, "Online Services."*

- If address or Direct Deposit information changes.

- If child's citizenship or immigration status changes.

- If child leaves the U.S. for 30 or more consecutive days.

- If child (or any beneficiary) dies or a disabled adult child receiving Social Security becomes unable to handle their benefits.

- If child starts working or is expected to have a change in earnings previously reported.

- If custody for the child changes.

- If post-age 18 child stops attending high school or is no longer in full-time attendance.

- If child marries.

- If the wage earner and stepchild's parent divorce.

- If the child is receiving as a disabled adult child and has a medical recovery allowing the possibility of a return to work.

- If a disabled adult child begins working (for wages or as a self-employed person), expected earnings must be reported promptly.

- If post-age 13 child has an unsatisfied warrant for at least 30 days for a felony.

- If child is confined for at least 30 continuous days to a jail, prison, penal institution or correctional facility for conviction of a crime.

- If child is confined to a public institution by court order for conviction of a crime.

Chapter 7

Filing for Supplemental Security Income (SSI)

Supplemental Security Income (SSI) is a federal program that provides financial assistance to people of limited income and resources. It is administered by the Social Security Administration. Some states increase the SSI payment by adding what is called a "state supplement." The Social Security Administration will explain the supplement if it is available in your state. The *federal* program rules and amounts are covered in this section.

When you file for Social Security benefits at age 65 (or older) and/or Disability Benefits, you are screened for SSI Aged Benefits and/or SSI Disability Benefits. If you are approved for Social Security benefits and meet the income and resource requirements for SSI, you could receive the difference between your Social Security benefit amount and the SSI benefit amount. It is important to make the distinction between Social Security Disability Benefits and SSI Disability Benefits. The Social Security Disability Benefit is referred to as *SSDI*. The Supplemental Security Income Disability Benefit is referred to as *SSIDI*. Some people will be eligible for benefits under both programs.

Because SSI is payable to only those who meet certain income and resource criteria, there are other programs that SSI beneficiaries automatically qualify for. The Claims Specialist who handles your claim can advise you of those programs or you may contact your local social service agency. If you are communicating with a social service agency, be sure to identify which type of disability (SSDI or SSIDI, or both) that you are receiving. This can eliminate a lot of confusion.

Requirements
- You must be a U.S. citizen, a resident of the Northern Mariana Islands, or lawfully residing in the U.S. *Some exceptions apply*. Access details at **www.socialsecurity.gov**. Select "Search" feature and type "Spotlight on SSI Benefits for Aliens." You may also call Social Security's 800# service.
- You must be at least age 65, or
- You must be blind or partially blind, or
- You must meet the Social Security definition for adult disability, or
- You must meet the requirements for a disabled child if applying as a child.
- Your income cannot exceed the monthly SSI amount payable ($20 exclusion allowed).
- Your resources must be within certain limits. (Your home does not count as a resource).

The benefit amounts listed below are the maximum payable under SSI. Other income, such as Social Security benefits, earnings, or other pensions, <u>will reduce</u> the amount of SSI payable.

SSI Monthly Federal Payment Amounts for 2019
- Individual $ 771
- Couple $1157

Resources/Assets allowed
- Individual $2000
- Couple $3000

When to Apply
File your application when you meet the requirements listed on page 29.

How to Apply (online, by phone, or in office)
- **Online** at www.socialsecurity.gov if the following criteria are met
  - Never been married
  - Not blind
  - U.S. citizen residing in one of the 50 states, District of Columbia, or the Northern Mariana Islands
  - Never applied for or received SSI benefits in the past
  - Applying for Social Security Disability at the same time as your SSI
- **Call** SSA at 1-800-772-1213 (TTY 1-800-325-0778). The 800# service will schedule an appointment with your local Social Security office. You can request an in-office (in-person interview) or a phone appointment.
- **Visit** your local Social Security office. To avoid a long wait, it is best to schedule an appointment.

Be Prepared to Answer Questions Regarding the Following and Provide Proof if Requested
- Identifying information: date of birth, place of birth, and address
- If not a U.S. citizen, your immigration status
- If lawfully admitted for permanent residence, details on admission to the U.S., and sponsorship if applicable
- Military Service dates
- Railroad service (if five years or longer)
- If you were outside the U.S. within 30 days prior to filing your application
- Unsatisfied felony warrants of any kind
- Marriages: Provide details on all marriages including dates of marriage and divorce (if currently married and residing with your spouse, all questions involving living arrangement, income, resources and expenses also apply to your spouse)
- Living arrangement: Alone or with someone or in supervised care facility (i.e., group home, hospital, retirement home, jail, rehab center, etc.)
- Details regarding your living arrangement i.e. cost of sharing a space with someone else
- Any help you receive in paying your expenses
- Resources/Assets such as life insurance policies, bank accounts, investment accounts, houses, buildings, land, cars, boats, and motorcycles, etc.
- Details regarding a transfer of title to property and/or details regarding money given away in the last 36 months
- Money or assets set aside for burial expenses
- All sources of income
- If you have worked or been self-employed, provide details including the rate of pay
- Your eligibility for SNAP (Supplemental Nutrition Assistance Program), also known as Food Stamps
- The date you became disabled, unless you are filing based on age (65 or older)

- If you are filing for Disability Benefits as an adult, you will be required to complete a *Disability Report Form, SSA-3368* which requires the following information:
  - o Your highest grade of education
  - o Vocational training (if any)
  - o Your job history for the last 15 years prior to your disability
  - o Types of machinery, technical skills or writing skills required in your job(s)
  - o How much time you spent doing physical activity – standing, walking, lifting, climbing
  - o How much weight you had to lift in your jobs
  - o Supervisory responsibilities
  - o Medications you take – dosage and reason for the medication
  - o Names, addresses, and phone numbers of doctors and dates of visits
  - o Names and dates of medical tests
- If you are applying for a child, provide details on schooling (if applicable), and complete a *Questionnaire for Children Claiming SSI Benefits, Form SSA-3881BK*. This form gathers information to determine the child's health care needs such as physical, speech, and occupational therapies; the child's activities at school; medications the child is taking; and the degree of care the child requires.
  Note: If filing for a child, income and resources of the parent(s) are required.

Submitting copies of medical records from doctors will help expedite the decision on your claim. You do not, however, have to obtain these records. The Disability Determination Services (DDS), a state agency that makes the medical decision for your disability claim, will assume responsibility for obtaining all medical records you list on your medical report *Form SSA-3368 or SSA-3881BK*.

You will be required to sign a form giving the Social Security Administration authorization to obtain your medical records from your health care providers. This form is called an *Authorization to Disclose Information to the Social Security Administration (SSA-827)*. You will usually be asked to sign one of these forms for each medical professional listed on your medical questionnaire plus two more. *You may also sign the SSA-827 online by attesting to an electronic signature.*

The more detail you provide on your medical report form, the sooner your decision will be made. If you have any paperwork from your doctor(s) or any lab work, you may include copies with your application. Also, it is very important to include details of your work history on the SSA-3368. See information above regarding the completion of the *Form SSA-3368*.

If you go to any new doctors after you file your application, you should let the Social Security Administration know. Social Security will notify the Disability Determination Service to update your record for new medical providers. If you return to work while your claim is pending, you must notify the Social Security Administration immediately.

The DDS might also schedule an appointment for you to see a doctor for a Consultative Examination (CE). You will be notified by mail of appointment details. The Social Security Administration will pay all medical costs associated with the appointment. *See Chapter 8, pp. 34-55, "Disability Benefits."*

Other Factors to Consider

Supplemental Security Income (SSI) beneficiaries who want to return to work have access to a number of incentives to help them become more independent.

Earnings Exclusion. In addition to a $20 general exclusion that can be allowed before the monthly SSI benefit is reduced, there is a formula to reduce the face value of gross earnings. For someone who is working, the gross earnings are reduced by $65 (earnings exclusion), then only one-half of the difference affects the monthly SSI benefit .

For example: Walter is receiving the maximum SSI benefit of $771 per month (for 2019). He has no other income. He goes to work and in his first month, earns $200 in gross wages. The $200 amount is reduced by the $20 general exclusion. This results in $180 which is then reduced by the $65 earned exclusion resulting in $115.00. Only one-half of the $115 is counted against Walter's monthly SSI benefit. This would reduce his SSI benefit by $57.50 resulting in a monthly SSI payment of $713.50.

Impairment Related Work Expenses (IRWEs). If you try to work while receiving Social Security and/or SSI Disability Benefits, you may qualify for IRWEs. This means that if you pay out-of-pocket for certain items necessary to permit you to work, you might be able to reduce the face value of your gross earnings. Some examples are transportation to and from work (if unable to drive yourself), counseling/training services, service animals, and special computer applications.

Plan to Achieve Self-Support (PASS). If you are receiving Supplemental Security Income (SSI) for a disability and want to try to work, the Social Security Administration can help you develop a (PASS) Plan to Achieve Self-Support. There are many incentives within the PASS program to help you reach your goal for independence. Make an appointment with your local Social Security office to meet with a Claims Specialist. You may schedule your appointment by calling 1-800-772-1213 (TTY 1-800-325-0778).

Ticket to Work. This is a program designed to help Social Security and SSI beneficiaries go to work at a job that might become full-time and permanent. During this time, you may keep your health insurance through Medicare and/or Medicaid. Social Security works in alliance with employment service providers called Employment Networks. This presents a great opportunity for you to find a job that can help you regain and maintain your independence. For information, call the Ticket to Work hotline (toll free) at 1-866-968-7842 (TTY 1-866-833-2967) or visit their website at www.choosework@ssa.gov.

Changes to Report (Supplemental Security Income)

Any of the following changes should be reported to Social Security immediately. Failure to do so could cause future benefits to be delayed or could result in an overpayment that you would have to repay. You may call 1-800-772-1213 (TTY 1-800-325-0778).

- Address change.
- You are admitted to or released from a hospital, nursing home, jail, prison or other correctional facility.
- You leave the U.S. for 30 consecutive days.
- Immigration status changes.
- You are no longer a legal resident of the U.S.
- Change in household members (someone moves in or out).
- Change in your share of household expenses.
- Birth or death of people with whom you live.
- Death of your spouse or former spouse.
- You divorce or separate from your spouse.
- You begin living with someone else as husband and wife.
- All changes in income for you and your spouse or parents:
  - Receive money from someone else
  - Start or stop work (keep all pay stubs)
  - Become eligible for another type of benefit
  - Win a lottery
  - Begin receiving child support
- Assistance you receive from other people. Provide details if it is money, food, or payment toward your household expenses.
- If your resources (things you own) go over $2000 as an individual, or $3000 as a couple.
- You sell or give anything of value away.
- Your disability improves.
- You start or stop school (if under age 22).
- If a warrant has been issued for your arrest.

If you are the parent, stepparent or representative payee for a child under age 18, report:
- A change in income for the child, his or her parents, or other family members in the household.
- A change in student status for siblings of the child who is receiving SSI.
- A change in the parents' or stepparents' marriage, residence, or resources.

Chapter 8

<u>Disability Benefits</u>

Requirements

- You must meet insured status requirements. See details below.
- You must meet Social Security's definition of disability. See details below.
- If filing as a Disabled Adult Child (DAC) on the record of a parent, you must be found disabled before age 22. The wage earner must meet insured status requirements.
- If filing as a Disabled Widow(er) or Disabled Surviving Divorced Spouse, you must be found disabled within seven years of the deceased wage earner's death. The deceased wage earner must meet insured status requirements.

Current Insured Status	Credits Required
Disabled before age 24	You must have 1.5 years of work (6 credits) during the 3-year period prior to your disability onset.
Between ages 24 and 31	You must have credits equaling one-half of the number of calendar quarters (4 quarters in a year) for the period between your 21st birthday and the calendar quarter in which you become disabled.
Age 31 or later	You must have 40 credits for fully insured status (20 of the credits must be in the 10-year period prior to the onset of your disability).
Special Insured Status exists for blind workers, for people who had a previous period of disability, and for some alien workers who were assigned Social Security numbers after January 1, 2004. Call Social Security's 800# service to verify qualifications.	

Definition of Social Security Disability. You have a condition, or combination of health issues, considered severe enough to prevent you from working at the "Substantial Gainful Activity" (SGA) level for 12 months or longer or the disability is expected to result in death. SGA is measured by the ability to work and earn a certain amount each month. Also considered are your age, your education, and your work history. It is a combination of these factors (health, age, education and work history) that determines your ability to work. While you may not be able to do your previous job, if you have the ability to do some other type of work, it could result in a denial of your claim. *See Table 2, p. 42 for SGA amounts.*

> **Example**: If you are a Certified Public Accountant and your disability necessitates use of a walker, you might still be able to do your job as a CPA or a different desk job. If, however, you are a brick layer and are found to have an inability to walk and are beyond a certain age with little training or education to do any other type of work, you might be approved for Disability Benefits.

When to Apply
File an application if you or your doctor believe you meet Social Security's definition of disability.

How to Apply (online, by phone, or in office)
- **Online** at www.socialsecurity.gov. The convenience of this is that you do not have to wait for an appointment. Due to the demand for appointments, it might be several weeks before one can be scheduled. If you complete your application online, you may use the "Remarks" section of the online application to request that a Claims Specialist call you to answer any questions you might have. See filing instructions below.
  - **Online Filing Instructions**
    - Access www.socialsecurity.gov/applyonline. You will see a screen listing the different types of benefits that can be filed online. Select the application type you want to file. You will be prompted through a series of screens (similar to pages of a paper application).
    - Answer questions as instructed. If you cannot answer timely, return to it later.
    - If you are inactive on a page for more than 25 minutes, you will receive a warning. You may request an extension (up to three times). You will then time out unless you resume answering questions. If you cannot complete the application in a single session, you may save it and *"Return to a Saved Application"* later without losing your information.
    - You will receive instructions at the end of a completed application telling you what your next steps are.
- **Call** SSA at 1-800-772-1213 (TTY 1-800-325-0778). The 800# service will schedule an appointment with your local Social Security office. You can request an in-office (in-person interview) or a phone appointment.
- **Visit** your local Social Security office. To avoid a long wait, it is best to schedule an appointment by calling the 800# service.

Be Prepared to Answer Questions Regarding
- The date you became disabled
- When and where you last worked
- Total amount of earnings in the previous and current years
- Military Service dates
- Workers' Compensation entitlement dates and amounts
- Work history or pension that was not covered by Social Security taxes
- Work performed in another country that has a social security program
- Work for the Railroad if more than five years
- Children under age 18, under age 19 and still a full-time student in high school or disabled before age 22. S*ee Chapter 6, pp. 26-28, "Children's Benefits."*
- Unsatisfied warrants
- Current marriage:
  - Name of spouse (including maiden name if applicable)
  - Social Security number (if known)
  - Date of birth
  - Date and city of marriage
    Note: If spouse is at least age 62, *see Chapter 3, pp. 10-14, "Spouse's Benefits."*

- Previous marriage(s):
    - Name of spouse (including maiden name if applicable)
    - Social Security number (if known)
    - Date of birth
    - Date and city of marriage
    - Date and city of divorce and/or death (if marriage ended with death of spouse)
      Note: If marriage ended in divorce, *see Chapter 4, pp. 15-19, "Divorced Spouse's Benefits."* If marriage ended in death, *see Chapter 5, pp. 20-25, "Survivor Benefits."*
      Additionally, if you are in a common-law marriage, or had a common-law marriage, call Social Security's 800# service to ask if your state recognizes common-law marriage.
- *Form SSA-3368 (Disability Report Form for adults) or Form SSA-3820 (Disability Report Form for adult child)* will require the following information
    - Vocational training (if any)
    - Your job history for the 15 year period prior to your disability
    - Types of machinery, technical skills or writing skills required in your jobs
    - How much time you spent doing physical activity – standing, walking, lifting, climbing
    - How much weight you had to lift in your jobs
    - Supervisory responsibilities
    - Medications you take – dosage and reason
    - Names, addresses, and phone numbers of doctors who have been treating you
    - First and last date you saw each doctor and dates for future appointments
    - Names and dates of medical tests

Documents That May be Required to Process your Application

- Birth Certificate
- Proof of Citizenship or lawful alien status if not a U.S. citizen
- Military Service Discharge (DD-214)
- W-2 form and/or self-employment tax return from previous year
- Workers' Compensation letter
- Bank information – name of financial institution, routing number, and account number
  If you do not have a bank account, the benefits can be set up on a prepaid debit card. See www.GoDirect.org.
  Note: Social Security can access some proofs online and will not need those proofs from you. If you need to submit proofs, you will be notified. Social Security will copy and return them to you by mail.

Submitting copies of medical reports from doctors will help expedite the decision on your claim. You are not, however, required to obtain such copies. The Disability Determination Services (DDS), a state agency that makes the medical decision on your disability claim, will assume responsibility for obtaining all medical information you list on your medical report *Form SSA-3368 or Form SSA-3820*. Be sure to answer questions thoroughly regarding your work history. The more details you provide on your medical report form, the sooner your decision will be made. If the state agency must contact you to update missing information, it will likely cause a delay in the decision on your claim. The DDS might also schedule an appointment for you to see a doctor for a Consultative Examination (CE). You will be notified by mail of your appointment details. The Agency will pay the medical costs associated with the appointment.

You will need to sign a form giving the Social Security Administration authorization to obtain your medical records from your health care providers. This form is called an *Authorization to Disclose Information to the Social Security Administration, SSA-827*. You will usually be asked to sign one for each medical professional listed on your medical questionnaire *Form SSA-3368 or Form SSA-3820* plus two more. You may sign the *Form SSA-827* online by acknowledging an electronic signature.

Note: If you go to any new doctors after you file your application, let Social Security know. They will notify the Disability Determination Service to update your record. If you return to work while your claim is pending, you must notify Social Security immediately.

Disability Decision

It can take from two to six months, depending on the type of disability, for a medical decision to be issued. When the state agency completes the review of your disability claim, your records are returned to your local Social Security office. You will receive a letter from the Social Security Administration notifying you of the decision.

- **If approved,** the letter will inform you of the date the state agency found you disabled, the date your benefits will begin (or should have begun), the amount of your benefits and the amount of retroactive benefits, if any, you are due. Often by the time a disability claim is approved, retroactive benefits are due on the record. You will be informed of your appeal rights should you disagree with any of the findings.
  Very Important: If you are approved and have children and/or a spouse who are eligible, contact the Social Security Administration promptly to schedule an appointment to file applications for them. See Chapter 3, pp. 10-14, "Spouse's Benefits;" & Chapter 6, pp. 26-28, "Children's Benefits."

- **If denied,** or you disagree with the date they found you disabled, you may file an appeal. Your appeal rights will be explained in the letter. Be aware that you have only 60 days in which to file the appeal. The 60 days begins five days after the date on the notice. *See Chapter 10, pp. 71-73, "Appeals Process."*

How Your Disability Benefit is Calculated – Social Security employees rely on computer software to do this calculation as it can be somewhat complex. You may get an estimate of your potential disability benefit by setting up an online account. See instructions on Page 2, "Create a Personal Account." The basic formula is shown below.

Step 1
Social Security determines how many years to use in the computation of disability benefits by first counting the number of years beginning with age 22 and ending with the year before your disability begins.

Step 2
The total years determined in Step 1 is divided by the number 5 and rounded down.

Step 3
The total in Step 1 is then reduced by the number of years calculated in Step 2 (not to exceed 5 years).

The result in Step 3 above equals the number of years that will be indexed for inflation and used to determine the Average Indexed Monthly Earnings (AIME) and finally the Primary Insurance Amount (PIA). *See Chapter 9, p. 56, "PIA Calculation."*

Other Factors to Consider

Waiting Period. There is a full five-month waiting period before Social Security Disability Benefits can be payable. For example, if the disability onset is established as March 15, 2018, the first full month would be April 2018. That begins the five-month waiting period. September would be the first month for which Disability Benefits would be payable. The first benefit is paid the month after it is due. The September benefit would be issued in October 2018. If, however, the disability onset is established as March 1, 2018, the first full month would be March 2018. August would be the first month for which Disability Benefits would be payable. The August check would be issued in September 2018.

Medicare Coverage. Medicare coverage, with some exceptions, will not begin until you have been entitled to 24 months of Social Security Disability Benefits. You will be mailed a Medicare card a month or two before your coverage begins. You do not have to recontact Social Security to file for it. However, you do need to consider enrolling in a Medicare Prescription Drug Plan (Part D) and a Supplemental Medicare Plan (Medigap). *See Chapter 11, pp. 74-91, "Medicare;" & Chapter 12, pp. 92-96, "Supplemental Medicare Insurance."*

Windfall Elimination Provision (WEP). If you are eligible for a pension from another agency, i.e., the Federal Government or an employer for which you did not pay Social Security taxes, your Social Security benefit could be reduced. This is called the Windfall Elimination Provision (WEP). This is a complex formula that reduces the Primary Insurance Amount (PIA) and will be calculated at the time you file your Social Security claim. You can also use the online calculator at www.socialsecurity.gov to figure your benefit amount.
Note: The WEP formula is not used for survivor benefits. *See Chapter 9, p. 57, "WEP Calculation."*

Workers' Compensation. If you are paid workers' compensation while receiving a Social Security disability benefit, your Social Security benefit will be offset. If you are paid a one-time lump sum workers' compensation benefit, it will be calculated as a monthly benefit for the prescribed worker's compensation period. The formula for offset is based on your average current earnings (ACE). The Social Security Administration will do the calculation if/when you are approved for Social Security Disability Benefits.

Supplemental Security Income (SSI). SSI is a federal benefit program that provides financial assistance to people of limited income and resources who meet Social Security's definition of disability or aged benefits (age 65 or older). If your Social Security Disability Benefit is below the SSI threshold, and you meet the other requirements, you should file an application for SSI based on disability at the same time you file for Social Security Disability Benefits.
Note: There is no five-month waiting period for SSI Disability Benefits. *See Chapter 7, pp. 29-33, "Supplemental Security Income."*

Impairment Related Work Expenses (IRWEs). If you try to work while receiving Social Security Disability Benefits, you may qualify for IRWEs. This means that if you must pay out-of-pocket for items necessary to make it possible for you to work, you might be able to reduce the face value of your gross earnings. Some examples are service animals, transportation to and from work (if unable to drive yourself), counseling/training services, special computer applications, etc. IRWEs are considered only if you continue to work after the 9-month Trial Work Period (TWP) has ended. *See pp. 41-43, "Trial Work Period."*

Changes to Report (Disability Benefits)

Important: Any of the following changes that occur after you start receiving benefits should be reported promptly. Failure to do so could cause future benefits to be delayed or could result in an overpayment that you would have to repay. You may call Social Security at 1-800-772-1213 (TTY 1-800-325-0778) or, if you have set up a personal account at www.socialsecurity.gov/myaccount, you may report most of your changes through your online account. You may also request your change by mail or visit your local Social Security office. *See Chapter 1, pp. 1-3, "Online Services."*

- Change of address, and/or Direct Deposit Information.

- You return to work (as an employee or a self-employed person) regardless of earnings amount.

- Your condition improves.

- You begin to receive workers' compensation (including a lump sum payment) and/or if the workers' compensation stops.

- You become entitled to a pension, annuity, public disability benefit or receive a lump sum payment based on employment for which you did not pay Social Security taxes.

- Change in citizenship or immigration status.

- You leave the U.S. for 30 or more consecutive days.

- Change in marital status (marriage, divorce, or annulment).

- You become the parent of a child (including an adopted child) after you filed your claim.

- Change in status for someone you have filed for or are caring for: if they leave your care, die, or if you lose custody.

- If you and the parent of a stepchild receiving on your Social Security record get a divorce.

- Issues involving possible criminal behavior:

  ➤ You have an unsatisfied warrant for 30 continuous days or longer for a parole or probation violation.
  ➤ You have a warrant for your arrest for a crime or attempted crime that is a felony.
  ➤ You are confined to a jail, prison, penal institution or correctional facility for more than 30 continuous days for conviction of a crime.
  ➤ You are confined to a public institution by court order in connection with a crime.

Continuing Disability Review (CDR)

If you are approved for Disability Benefits, a medical re-exam diary is set on your record. This means that at some point your case will be selected for a medical review. The review is usually initiated three to seven years after your benefits start. This review is called a *Continuing Disability Review (CDR)*. A CDR could occur sooner if there is a report of medical recovery or a return to work.

If your case is selected for review, you will likely receive a form from the Social Security Administration asking you to provide updated information on your medical condition. It could be a Form SSA-455 (hard paper form) or a Form SSA-455-OCR-SM (scannable mailer form). The forms are self-explanatory. Complete the form and return it in the self-addressed/stamped envelope provided. If you have a record of the medical information you provided when you filed your application for disability, you can refer to your list of doctors and their contact information *but be sure to list any new health problems, new doctors and new medications.* Please complete the form thoroughly and return it promptly.

The Social Security Administration will review your completed form to determine if they need to schedule you for a full medical CDR. If so, you will be sent a notice with instructions of what to do. Your benefits will continue uninterrupted until the medical review is completed. The medical reviews are not done by the Social Security Administration. A state agency known as Disability Determination Services (DDS) is responsible for the decision.

If you are notified that your medical condition has improved, and that you are now able to return to work, your notice will include the date that your benefits are going to stop or should have stopped. If you disagree with the decision, you may file an appeal. Follow the instructions in your Social Security notice regarding what kind of appeal you can file. The first appeal is usually called a Reconsideration *(Form SSA-789)*. In addition to the *Form SSA-789*, you must complete the appropriate medical questionnaire *Form SSA-3441* for an adult, *Form SSA-3881* for a child/adult child, and medical release *Forms SSA-827.* The Reconsideration request is sent back to DDS (the state agency that makes the medical decisions) where it is reviewed by someone who was not involved in the original decision. **If you want your benefits to continue while your disability cessation is being reconsidered, you must file the Reconsideration within 10 days and include a written request for the benefits to continue.** Otherwise, you have 60 days from the date you receive the notice in which to file a Reconsideration.

If you file a Reconsideration and it is denied, you may then file a Hearing *(Form SSA-501)* which is a request for review by an Administrative Law Judge (ALJ). Some states allow you to skip filing a Reconsideration and go directly to the Hearing level. Your Social Security notice will instruct you regarding the appropriate appeal to file. **If you want your benefits to continue while awaiting a decision on your Hearing, you must file your request within 10 days.** Otherwise, you have 60 days from the date you receive the notice in which to file the Hearing request. If the Hearing is denied, you have the right to file for a review by the Appeals Council.

Very Important: Be aware that choosing to have your benefits continue while awaiting your appeal could result in an overpayment if the appeal is denied. *See Chapter 14, p. 98, "Overpayments."*

Trial Work Period (TWP)

This is good news for those receiving Social Security Disability Benefits who want to try to return to work. Since the definition of a Social Security disability is the inability to perform Substantial Gainful Activity (SGA), a return to work puts the person at risk of losing what is possibly his/her only income. Substantial Gainful Activity is defined as having the ability to work and earn a certain amount each month. *See Table 2, p. 42 for SGA amounts.*

The Social Security Administration allows a nine-month period in which a beneficiary can work without any limit on his/her monthly earnings and still receive Social Security benefits for those months. This is called the Trial Work Period (TWP) and it is available to anyone receiving Social Security Disability Benefits *(not Supplemental Security Income benefits)*. The nine months in which you attempt to work at the Substantial Gainful Activity level do not have to be consecutive. The nine months of work at the SGA level must occur during a *rolling* 60-month period. This means the Trial Work Period will end once you have worked at the SGA level during a 60-month period.

You must notify the Social Security Administration when you return to work. Then, you must keep a record of any month you work and earn over the TWP limit. You will be required to submit your pay stubs at the time of your review. Keep them in an envelope or folder for easy access. If you are self-employed, the number of hours you work in a month is also a factor – 80 hours or more may indicate an ability to return to work. If you are self-employed, speak with a Social Security Claims Specialist regarding your work situation. *See Table 1, p. 42 for TWP amounts.*

You will continue to have Medicare coverage during your Trial Work Period. In fact, your Medicare Part A and B coverage can continue 93 months after the Trial Work Period ends unless you have had a medical recovery. You must continue to pay your Part B premium. You will be billed quarterly for the premium. Beyond the 93-month period, you may purchase Medicare Part A and B if you still have a disabling condition. *See Chapter 11, pp. 74-91, "Medicare."*

Once you have completed the ninth month of your Trial Work Period, your ability to return to work will be reviewed. If there is a finding that you can work and perform Substantial Gainful Activity (SGA), your Social Security benefits will be suspended.

You will have a grace period in which you will receive two additional months of benefits after the ninth month. That means you will receive a benefit for the ninth month plus two more. **Beyond that, any benefits you receive for months in which you earn at or above the SGA amount will likely be considered an overpayment and will need to be repaid to Social Security.** *See Chapter 14, p. 98, "Overpayments."*

If you report a return to work but stop before completing your nine months, let the Social Security Administration know. Any changes should be reported promptly.

Tracking your Earnings
Keep a personal record of your earnings so that you know when your Trial Work Period ends. See the TWP Worksheet designed to aid you in tracking your earnings, *(TWP Worksheet, pp. 109-110).* You may photocopy that worksheet to help you understand when your benefits should stop. Also, included in this chapter is an example of how the worksheet is to be used. *See pp. 44-48, "Trial Work Period Case Example."*

Earnings Tolerances for Disability Beneficiaries
Trial Work Month is defined as a month in which a disability beneficiary works and has earnings at levels shown below. This table shows the monthly Trial Work Period earning amounts beginning with 2010.

Table 1	
Trial Work Period – *Gross* Monthly Earnings	
2010 - $720	2015 - $780
2011 - $720	2016 - $810
2012 - $720	2017 - $840
2013 - $750	2018 - $850
2014 - $770	2019 - $880

You need to be aware of these amounts if you return to work. After the ninth month (in a 60-month period) of work and earnings at the Trial Work Period level, your case will be reviewed for your ability to work and earn at the Substantial Gainful Activity level. You may obtain amounts for years not listed in Table 1 or Table 2 online at www.socialsecurity.gov or by calling 1-800-772-1213 (TTY 1-800-325-0778).

An ability to engage in Substantial Gainful Activity (SGA) means you can maintain employment at a certain earnings level. Below is a table of the monthly SGA earning amounts beginning with 2010. The SGA thresholds for blind beneficiaries are higher. Contact Social Security to discuss the earnings amounts allowed along with other work incentives for the blind.

Table 2	
Substantial Gainful Activity – *Gross* Monthly Earnings	
2010 - $1000	2015 - $1090
2011 - $1000	2016 - $1130
2012 - $1010	2017 - $1170
2013 - $1040	2018 - $1180
2014 - $1070	2019 - $1220

The takeaway here is that while you might have earnings high enough to cause your nine-month Trial Work Period to expire, you still might be under the SGA earnings level. If that is the case, you could continue to be entitled to Disability Benefits, assuming you have not had a medical recovery. However, *at any point beyond the Trial Work Period that you start to earn at the SGA level, your* <u>*entitlement*</u> *to Disability Benefits will end.*

Unfortunately, because of the time involved in reviewing this type of case and the mounting demands on Social Security employees, it can take Social Security six months to two years (and sometimes longer) to complete a full review. If, after the review, the final decision is that you are (or have been) performing at the SGA level, the benefits you received beyond the Trial Work Period and the two-month grace period will be considered an overpayment and will have to be repaid to Social Security. It is very rare that an overpayment of this type can be waived. *If you continue to work at the SGA level after your Trial Work Period ends, you should start saving the Social Security benefits you receive.* Once Social Security has completed its review of your case, you will be notified by Social Security to repay benefits you were not due. *See Chapter 14, p. 98, "Overpayments."*

Problems often occur if a beneficiary confuses the amount of earnings allowed for Retirement Benefits versus earnings allowed for Disability Benefits. **The rules for work and earnings while receiving Retirement Benefits are very different from the rules for Social Security Disability Benefits.** To read how earnings affect Retirement Benefits, *see Chapter 9, p. 61, "Earnings Test;" & pp. 62-64, "Earnings Test Examples."*

People receiving Supplemental Security Income (SSI) sometimes confuse the rules for Social Security Disability with SSI Disability. **The rules for those receiving SSI are very different in that all income received may reduce or prevent payment of SSI benefits.** For more details, you may contact Social Security at 1-800-772-1213 (TTY 1-800-325-0778) or go their website www.socialsecurity.gov.

On the following pages, I have included a case example of how work and earnings can affect benefits. Also included is a completed worksheet to show you how to track your earnings and benefits. This will help you know what benefits you are due and at what point benefits should be retained in case they have to be repaid to the Social Security Administration.

Trial Work Period/Extended Period of Eligibility Case Example

TWP Case Facts

John became eligible for Social Security Disability Benefits effective October 2010. He had been receiving benefits for almost two years when he decided to try working again. Because John was not sure if he was medically ready, he started by working part time.

John began working several hours a week in June 2012.

He worked June, July, and August and earned $900 each month in gross earnings.

He then stopped work and did not return until January 2013.

He worked only one week and earned $490 in January.

He returned to work in July 2013. He worked three months but earned only $670 per month.

John had surgery for a health issue and was off until January 2014, at which time he thought he was ready to work longer hours at his job. In January 2014 he earned $1200 but had a relapse and was not able to return to work again until February 2015. He was then given a job that was less physically demanding for him. He was able to maintain this job and earned $1800 per month for the next three years.

Reviewing John's TWP worksheet

The worksheet (*p. 47*) shows the first month John returns to work and earns over the allowable TWP month. It is possible that a person can return to work and have many months, if not years, of work under the TWP limits, in which case, you would not use this Worksheet. The Worksheet is only to be started after the first TWP month has been completed.

In June 2012, John earned $900 (gross). That amount exceeds the monthly $720 TWP limit thus his Trial Work Period begins. He repeats those earnings in July and August before he stops working. He has now used three trial work months. You need not complete every column or line of the worksheet but be sure to record earnings information for the months that you work.

In January 2013, John worked and earned $450 for that month. This amount is under the monthly TWP limit of $750 so that month is not counted as a trial work month.

John is off again until July 2013. He returns to work for three months (July, August and September) and earns $670 per month. His gross earnings are under the monthly $750 TWP limit, so those months do not count toward his Trial Work Period.

In January 2014, John worked for one month and earned $1200 gross wages. That exceeds the monthly TWP limit of $770. He has now completed another trial work month. This means he has now completed four trial work months. Reminder – he is due benefits for all months until he has completed his Trial Work Period.

In February 2015, John returned to work after having a setback. He begins earning $1800 in gross wages every month. In June 2015, he completes his Trial Work Period. That is the 9th month (in a 60-month period) in which his earnings meet the TWP limit. He is due his benefit for the following two months (July and August). If he receives a benefit for September (which would be paid in October), he will not be due that benefit or benefits for any of the following months unless he drops below the SGA amount. Keep in mind the benefits are paid the month after they are due.

Trial Work Period Worksheet Instructions

Month & Year of Work

In the first block, record the month and year for your first month of earnings that equal or exceed the Trial Work Period monthly amount. For TWP amounts, *see Table 1, p. 42.* Fill in the following 60 blocks with the months and years that follow. Continue to record your gross earnings for months in which you work. If you have months in which you did not work, you may leave it blank or enter a zero.

Gross Earnings/SE Hours

Enter your gross earnings for all months in which you work. If self-employed, record the number of hours worked each month. If you know your approximate net earnings for the month, enter that amount.

TWP Amounts Allowed

Enter the TWP amounts allowed for all months in which you work. *See Table 1, p. 42.*

Your TWP Months

Identify numerically which months your earnings or self-employment hours equal or exceed the allowable amounts for a trial work month, e.g. 1, 2, or 3, etc. Once you have reached 9 trial work months in a 60-month period, you have completed your Trial Work Period.

SGA Monthly Amounts

Enter the Substantial Gainful Activity Amounts allowed for months in which you listed earnings. For SGA amounts, see *Table 2, p. 42.*

Months with SGA Earnings

Beginning with the first month after your 9-month Trial Work Period, enter earnings in this column for months which equal or exceed the SGA amount. For example, if you completed the 9th month of your Trial Work Period 30 months into the 60-month period, and were continuing to work at SGA, you would start to record your earnings effective with the 31st month. This would technically be the end of your entitlement to Disability Benefits but because Social Security allows two additional months of benefits, the earnings for those two months won't count against you. Be aware that you will receive a benefit for the 9th month plus two additional months (called grace months). Beyond that, all months in which you earn at the SGA amount or higher are months that you are NOT due a benefit. *See p. 9, "Extended Period of Eligibility."*

SS Benefit Received

Enter a "Y" (for yes) or "N" (for no) for all months in which you received a Social Security benefit. If unsure, refer to your bank statement (online or paper).

SS Benefit Due

Enter a "Y" (for yes) or "N" (for no) for all months in which you are due or not due a benefit. If you have received benefits for any months in which you have recorded an "N" (not due a benefit), consider saving those benefits. Although the Social Security Administration will be collecting earnings information through its record keeping systems such as employer reports and IRS tax systems, it is impossible for them to update your record monthly. Because of the lag time involved in collecting and reviewing the data, it could be months (sometimes 24 months or more) before the Social Security Administration notifies you that your benefits should cease or should have ceased. **This delay in rendering a decision does not relieve you of your responsibility to keep good records. It is important for you to know what benefits you are due and not due.**

After the Social Security Administration has done its review of your disability work record, you will be notified of the months for which you were not due a benefit. This often results in an overpayment notice being issued in which you will be asked to return the overpaid benefits to the Social Security Administration. Please note that although you have a right to file for a waiver of an overpayment, the rules for allowing a waiver are very defined and it is very, very rare that an overpayment due to earnings can be waived. *See Chapter 14, p. 98, "Overpayments."*

Trial Work Period Worksheet (Case Example for John)

	Month & Year of Work	Gross Earnings/ SE Hours	TWP Amounts Allowed	Your TWP Months used	SGA Monthly Amounts	Months with SGA Earnings	SS Benefit Received? Y or N	SS Benefit Due? Y or N
1	6/2012	$900	$720	1	$1010		Y	Y
2	7/2012	$900	↑	2	↑		Y	Y
3	8/2012	$900		3			Y	Y
4	9/2012	$0						
5	10/2012							
6	11/2012							
7	12/2012		↓		↓			
8	1/2013	$490	$750	---	$1040		Y	Y
9	2/2013		↑		↑			
10	3/2013							
11	4/2013							
12	5/2013							
13	6/2013							
14	7/2013	$670		---				
15	8/2013	$670		---				
16	9/2013	$670		---				
17	10/2013							
18	11/2013							
19	12/2013		↓		↓			
20	1/2014	$1200	$770	4	$1070		Y	Y
21	2/2014		↑		↑			
22	3/2014							
23	4/2014							
24	5/2014							
25	6/2014							
26	7/2014							
27	8/2014							
28	9/2014							
29	10/2014							
30	11/2014		↓		↓			

	Month & Year of Work	Gross Earnings/ SE Hours	TWP Amounts Allowed	Your TWP Months used	SGA Monthly Amounts	Months with SGA Earnings	SS Benefit Received? Y or N	SS Benefit Due? Y or N
31	12/2014							
32	1/2015		$780		$1090			
33	2/2015	$1800	↑	5	↑		Y	Y
34	3/2015	$1800		6			Y	Y
35	4/2015	$1800		7			Y	Y
36	5/2015	$1800		8			Y	Y
37	*6/2015*	*$1800*		*9*		*$1800*	*Y*	*Y*
38	*7/2015**	*$1800*		*10*		*$1800*	*Y*	*Y*
39	*8/2015*	*$1800*		*11*		*$1800*	*Y*	*Y*
40	**9/2015**	**$1800**				**$1800**	**Y**	**N**
41	**10/2015**	**$1800**				**$1800**	**Y**	**N**
42	**11/2015**	**$1800**				**$1800**	**Y**	**N**
43	**12/2015**	**$1800**	↓		↓	**$1800**	**Y**	**N**
44	**1/2016**	**$1800**	**$810**		**$1130**	**$1800**	**Y**	**N**
45	2/2016	$1800	↑		↑	$1800		
46	3/2016	$1800				$1800		
47	4/2016	$1800				$1800		
48	5/2016	$1800				$1800		
49	6/2016	$1800				$1800		
50	7/2016	$1800				$1800		
51	8/2016	$1800				$1800		
52	9/2016	$1800				$1800		
53	10/2016	$1800				$1800		
54	11/2016	$1800				$1800		
55	12/2016	$1800	↓		↓	$1800		
56	1/2017	$1800	$840		$1170	$1800		
57	2/2017	$1800	↑		↑	$1800		
58	3/2017	$1800				$1800		
59	4/2017	$1800				$1800		
60	5/2017	$1800	↓		↓	$1800		

Must have 9 TWP months in the 60-month period. Continue adding months until the 9th month occurs in a 60-month period.
*Extended Period of Eligibility begins the month after the TWP ends. See following instructions.

Extended Period of Eligibility (EPE)

Following the completion of the Trial Work Period, there is a 36-month period in which the Social Security Administration keeps your eligibility for benefits open in case you drop below the Substantial Gainful Activity (SGA) amounts in any month. *See Table 2, p. 42 for SGA amounts.* Remember, the amount that "counts" is the gross earnings unless you are self-employed. Self-employment will require more attention to detail in that the number of hours and your net earnings are counted. If you are self-employed, speak with a Claims Specialist at the Social Security Administration. Earnings from self-employment are much more difficult to track. You should get instruction from the Claims Specialist about your particular work situation.

Medicare Part A and B coverage can continue up to 93 months after the nine-month Trial Work Period ends as long as you are considered disabled. *See Chapter 11, pp. 74-91, "Medicare."*

Tracking your Earnings
Included in this chapter is an example of how the EPE worksheet is to be used to track your earnings. Keep a personal record of your earnings so that you know if and when you are due a benefit during the Extended Period of Eligibility (EPE). You may photocopy this worksheet and use it to help alert you to a possible overpayment of benefits.

During the EPE, if you receive benefits for any month in which your earnings equal or exceed the SGA amount, you will have to return those benefits. Keep them in savings. Once the Social Security Administration has done its review (which could be anywhere from 6 to 24 months or longer), you will be notified of how much you need to pay back to Social Security. Review the TWP and EPE case example worksheets included in this chapter. *See Table 1, p. 42 for TWP amounts.*

If you incur expenses necessary to allow you to work, some of those expenses might decrease the actual earnings that would count against you. These expenses are called Impairment Related Work Expenses (IRWEs). Some expenses that could be considered IRWEs are service animals, medical devices, special transportation to and from work, and modifications to your vehicle for work purposes. If you return to work and have out-of-pocket costs for anything that is necessary to support your ability to work, keep proof of all costs incurred and notify the Social Security Administration. *See Table 1, p. 42 for TWP amounts.*

Extended Period of Eligibility Worksheet Case Example

The Extended Period of Eligibility (EPE) case example worksheets on pages 52-53 correlate with the Trial Work Period (TWP) case example and worksheets for John on pages 44-48. See blank worksheets for the Extended Period of Eligibility to aid you in tracking months that you are due or not due benefits, *(EPE Worksheet, pp. 111-112)*. Recording your monthly earnings will keep you aware of the possibility of an overpayment. **You should try to save benefits paid to you for months you are not due Social Security.** *See Chapter 14, p. 98, "Overpayments."*

EPE Facts:
John continues to earn $1800 per month until December 2017.

John is due a Social Security disability benefit for June plus the two-month grace period (July and August). The benefits are paid the month after they are due so the benefit for August will be paid in September 2015. This means that any benefits John receives after September 2015 will be considered an overpayment. He should begin saving those benefits. He will likely have to repay them to the Social Security Administration.

In December 2017, John suffers a major setback and is struggling to remain at his job. His employer allows him to reduce his hours and he is now earning only $600 (gross) per month.

Because John is now in his Extended Period of Eligibility which began July 2015 (the month after his TWP ended), he should call the Social Security Administration at 1-800-772-1213 (TTY 1-800-325-0778) to report that his earnings have dropped below the SGA level. The Social Security Administration can reinstate his benefits for any month he is under the SGA level during the Extended Period of Eligibility.

Extended Period of Eligibility (EPE) Worksheet Instructions

See TWP Case Example. The instructions below correlate with the information entered on the TWP worksheets, *(pp. 47-48).*

Month & Year of Work

Using the EPE worksheet on pages 52-53, begin by entering the first month following the 9th trial work month. In the TWP case example for John (above), his 9th trial work month was 06/2015. That means 07/2015 is the first month to be entered on the EPE Worksheet. Remember, the EPE begins the first month following the 9th trial work month. List all months in chronological order for the next 35 months. Complete the remaining sheet as shown below.

SGA Amount Allowed

Enter the Substantial Gainful Activity (SGA) amounts allowed for the 36-month period. For SGA gross monthly earning amounts, s*ee Table 2, p. 42.*

Your Gross Earnings or Net Earnings and hours worked if self-employed

Enter your total gross earnings or net earnings and hours worked if self-employed for each month. Months that you are under the SGA amounts are months that you are eligible for benefits during your EPE. Any benefits received for months that you are <u>over</u> the SGA amount become an overpayment and will have to be repaid.

Are You Due Benefits?

Indicate "Y" for yes if you are due benefits and "N" for no if you are not due benefits. Refer to instructions above regarding gross earnings and self-employment.

EPE Worksheet Example (36 Month Period)

(See TWP Case Example Worksheet – pp. 47-48)

	Month & Year of Work	SGA Amount Allowed	Your Gross Earnings or SE Hours	Are you due benefits? Y or N
1	*7/2015**	*$1090*	*$1800*	*Y (Grace month)*
2	*8/2015*	↑	*$1800*	*Y (Grace month)*
3	9/2015		$1800	N
4	10/2015		$1800	N
5	11/2015		$1800	N
6	12/2015	↓	$1800	N
7	1/2016	$1130	$1800	N
8	2/2016	↑	$1800	N
9	3/2016		$1800	N
10	4/2016		$1800	N
11	5/2016		$1800	N
12	6/2016		$1800	N
13	7/2016		$1800	N
14	8/2106		$1800	N
15	9/2016		$1800	N
16	10/2016		$1800	N
17	11/2016		$1800	N
18	12/2016	↓	$1800	N
19	1/2017	$1170	$1800	N
20	2/2017	↑	$1800	N
21	3/2017		$1800	N
22	4/2017		$1800	N
23	5/2017		$1800	N
24	6/2017		$1800	N
25	7/2017		$1800	N
26	8/2017		$1800	N
27	9/2017		$1800	N
28	10/2017		$1800	N
29	11/2017	↓	$1800	N

	Month & Year of Work	SGA Amount Allowed	Your Gross Earnings or SE Hours	Are you due benefits? Y or N
30	12/2017		$600	Y
31	1/2018	$1180		
32	2/2018	▲		
33	3/2018			
34	4/2018			
35	5/2018			
36	6/2018	▼		

*EPE start date. Ends 36 months later.

Note: Any benefits you receive in a month in which you indicate an "N" will have to be returned to the Social Security Administration.

If John's gross earnings for December 2017 through June 2018 stay under the SGA amounts, he can be paid benefits for those months. However, if it is determined that he had a medical recovery at any point during his EPE, the benefits for all months following the medical recovery would have to be repaid to Social Security.

Expedited Reinstatement of Disability Benefits

Social Security allows an additional period *beyond* the 36-month EPE (Extended Period of Eligibility) in which you can have your Disability Benefits reinstated if you become unable to work at a Substantial Gainful Activity level. However, since you must still be considered disabled, the Disability Determination Service (DDS) will need to review your medical information. You can receive benefits for up to six months while the medical determination is in process. *If the DDS finds you are no longer disabled, the benefits you received during the additional six months will be considered an overpayment and will have to be repaid.*

If you become unable to work because of your disability at the Substantial Gainful Activity level (*Table 2, page 42*) within the five-year period following your EPE, contact the Social Security Administration. They will inform you if you meet the requirements to be reinstated.

If at any time during your Trial Work Period, the Extended Period of Eligibility, or the Expedited Reinstatement period, you have a medical recovery, you should notify the Social Security Administration. Medical recovery means you no longer meet the definition of disability and, therefore, you are not eligible for Social Security Disability Benefits.

Medicare coverage can continue for 93 months (7 years and 9 months) after the 9-month Trial Work Period *unless you have a medical recovery*. If you want to keep Part B of Medicare, you must continue to pay the monthly premium.

In summary (unless you have a medical recovery):

1st - You have a **9-month Trial Work Period (TWP)** in a "rolling" 60-month period.

2nd- You have a **36-month Extended Period of Eligibility (EPE)** that begins the month after your 9th trial work month.

3rd- You have a **five-year period beyond the 36-month EPE** in which your benefits could be reinstated if your earnings drop below the Substantial Gainful Activity level. A new medical review will be required.

Ticket to Work

This is a program designed to help Social Security beneficiaries go to work at a job that might become full-time and permanent. During this time, you may keep your health insurance through Medicare and/or Medicaid. Social Security works in alliance with employment service providers called Employment Networks.

Depending on your type of disability, you might receive a call from one of the Employment Networks to ask if you are interested in the Ticket to Work program. Your decision to participate is voluntary and there is no cost for the service they provide. There are numerous advantages for beneficiaries who participate in this program. Someone with the Employment Network or a Vocational Rehabilitation agency works with you to define your career goals, to develop an employment plan, and to review your progress.

This presents a great opportunity for you to find a job that can help you regain and maintain your independence. For information, call the Ticket to Work hotline (toll free) at 1-866-968-7842 (TTY 1-866-833-2967) or visit their website at www.choosework@ssa.gov.

Plan to Achieve Self-Support (PASS)

If you are receiving Supplemental Security Income (SSI) for a disability and want to return to work, the Social Security Administration can help you develop a Plan to Achieve Self-Support (PASS). There are many incentives within the PASS program to help you reach your goal for independence. Make an appointment with your local Social Security office to meet with a Claims Specialist. You may schedule your appointment by calling 1-800-772-1213 (TTY 1-800-325-0778).

Chapter 9

Social Security Benefit Calculations

Primary Insurance Amount (PIA)

The Primary Insurance Amount (PIA) must be calculated for every type of Social Security benefit. The calculation for the PIA also determines total family benefits payable. Some factors will vary depending on the type of benefit, *such as the number of years used* in the computation of retirement benefits versus disability or survivor benefits for younger wage earners.

Step 1 – Each year of earnings to be used is indexed (not beyond age 60 for Retirement Benefits). Indexing earlier years allows an adjustment for inflation that will result in a higher benefit. The formula to calculate Retirement Benefits always uses 35 years of earnings. The number of years used for disability and survivor benefits depends on the year of disability or death.

Step 2 – The earnings selected are added together. The sum is then divided by the appropriate divisor (i.e. the number of years used x 12 months). The result is the Average Indexed Monthly Earnings (AIME). The divisor for Retirement Benefits is always 420 (35 years x 12 months). The divisor for disability and survivor benefits is based on the wage earner's age at the time.

Step 3 – The AIME is then put through the following three-step formula. Each year, the value of the bend point (*monetary step in the formula*) can change. To do this manually, you would need the earnings history showing the indexed earnings for each year. The formula below is provided to show you how it is calculated. The online calculator at www.socialsecurity.gov will provide your indexed earnings and do this calculation for you. You may also call the 800# service.

Record your AIME (Money amounts below are bend points for 2019) = $XXXX
a-Multiply bend point of $926 in the AIME by 90%   _____
b-Multiply the amount over $926 (not to exceed $5583) by 32%   _____
c-Multiply the amount over $5583 (if any) by 15%   _____
d-Total a, b, & c   _____

The amount you list in "d" is your Primary Insurance Amount (PIA) rounded down to the nearest dime. This is the amount payable at your full retirement age.

Example using AIME of $2083	$2083.00
a-Multiply bend point of $926 in the AIME by 90%	833.40
b-Multiply the amount over $926 (not to exceed $5583) by 32%	370.24
($2083 minus $926 = $1157) $1157 x 32%	
c-Multiply the amount over $5583 (if any) by 15%	0.00
d-Total is Primary Insurance Amount (rounded down)	$1203.60

Rule of Thumb for Retirement Benefits – Your Retirement Benefit is about 40% of your average monthly working wage for a 35-year period.

Windfall Elimination Provision (WEP) Calculation

If you are eligible for a pension from another agency, i.e., the Federal Government or an employer where you did not pay Social Security taxes on your wages, your Social Security benefit could be reduced. This is called the Windfall Elimination Provision (WEP). This is a formula that reduces the Primary Insurance Amount (PIA) and will be calculated at the time you file your retirement claim. You can also use the calculator at **www.socialsecurity.gov/planners** to figure your benefit. *Note*: Survivor benefits are not affected by the Windfall Elimination Provision.

Refer to the example from the previous page on how to calculate a Social Security benefit. The steps to calculate the AIME are the same. Once the AIME is figured, the formula that applies percentages to certain bend points (money amount assigned) is where you see the change. The example below assumes the wage earner had no more than 20 years of covered Social Security work and, therefore, the first bend point is multiplied by 40% instead of 90%.

Step 1 – Each year of earnings is put through a formula called indexing to adjust the earnings to today's averages. Indexing your earlier years allows an adjustment for inflation that will result in a higher Social Security benefit.

Step 2 – The highest 35 years of earnings are selected and added together. The sum is then divided by 420 (35 years x 12 months). The result is your Average Indexed Monthly Earnings (AIME) over the 35-year period. These numbers could be much lower for a younger wage earner.

Step 3 – The AIME is then put through the following three step formula. Each year, the value of the bend point (monetary step in the formula) can change. The bend points below are for 2019. To do this calculation you would need your earnings history showing the indexed earnings for each year. This formula is provided to show you how it is done. You may access the online calculator at **www.socialsecurity.gov/planner** to compute your PIA. You may also call the 800# service.

Example using AIME of $2083	$2083.00
a-Multiply bend point of $926 in the AIME by 40%	370.40
b-Multiply the amount over $926 (not to exceed $5583) by 32%	370.24
($2083 minus $926 = $1157) $1157 x 32%	
c-Multiply the amount over $5583 (if any) by 15%	0.00
d-Total is Primary Insurance Amount (rounded down)	$740.60

The example above shows the first step of the AIME being multiplied by 40% instead of 90%. The percentage used in the first bend point is between 40% to 90% depending on the number of work years covered by Social Security taxes. For example, if the wage earner above had 25 years of covered work, the first percentage factor would be 65% instead of 40%. If a person continues to work and earn *substantial earnings*, it is possible the number of years could increase the first percentage factor in the formula, which would increase the PIA. To see a chart of substantial earnings, and how benefits are affected by the Windfall Elimination Provision (WEP), go to **www.socialsecurity.gov/planners/retire/wep-chart.html**.

Full Retirement Age (FRA)
Table 1

Full Retirement Age Table	
Year of Birth	Full Retirement Age
1943-1954	66
1955	66 and 2 months
1956	66 and 4 months
1957	66 and 6 months
1958	66 and 8 months
1959	66 and 10 months
1960 and later	67
Note: Anyone born on the first day of the month is deemed to have been born the month before.	

Survivor Benefits Full Retirement Age (FRA)
Table 2

Full Retirement Age Table for Widow/Widower/Surviving Divorced Spouse	
Date of Birth	Full Retirement Age
Before- 1/1/40	65
1/2/40 - 1/1/41	65 and 2 months
1/2/41 - 1/1/42	65 and 4 months
1/2/42 - 1/1/43	65 and 6 months
1/2/43 - 1/1/44	65 and 8 months
1/2/44 - 1/1/45	65 and 10 months
1/2/45 - 1/1/57	66
1/2/57 - 1/1/58	66 and 2 months
1/2/58 - 1/1/59	66 and 4 months
1/2/59 - 1/1/60	66 and 6 months
1/2/60 - 1/1/61	66 and 8 months
1/2/61 - 1/1/62	66 and 10 months
1/2/62 - or later	67
Note: Anyone born on the first day of the month is deemed to have been born the month before.	

Benefits - Age 62 vs Age 66 vs Age 70 Calculations

Deciding when to start your benefits is a very personal decision and often dependent on your financial situation. Some people want to delay starting their benefits until full retirement age (FRA) or until age 70 to earn Delayed Retirement Credits (see example on next page). Others make their decision based on the availability of health insurance. If your employer or your spouse's employer provides a health insurance plan after retirement, it is an easier decision; but if not, waiting until you qualify for Medicare at age 65 might be the better decision. Also, family longevity might be a factor to consider.

Below are two scenarios showing how your monthly benefit amount could look very different depending on the age at which you start benefits. You may check your benefits by establishing a personal account on Social Security's website at www.socialsecurity.gov/myaccount. The online calculators can provide you many different scenarios. You may also contact Social Security to speak with a Claims Specialist regarding your options. Social Security employees cannot, however, advise you of what to do.

Note: See Chapter 2, pp. 5-9, "Retirement Benefits;" Chapter 3, pp. 10-14, "Spouse's Benefits;" Chapter 4, pp. 15-19, "Divorced Spouse's Benefits;" & Chapter 5, pp. 20-25, "Survivor Benefits."

Scenario 1 - Comparing benefits at age 62 vs age 66 (Full Retirement Age - FRA)

The reduction factor for Social Security Retirement Benefits is 5/9 of 1% for the first 36 months and 1/12 of 1% for any additional months up to full retirement age. This example is for someone whose full retirement age is 66 resulting in a 25% reduction at age 62, The PIA would be reduced as follows:

Primary Insurance Amount at FRA (age 66)	$2000
Benefits are reduced by 25% at age 62	x75%
Monthly Benefit Amount (MBA)	$1500

To calculate the advantage of starting your benefit before FRA, multiply $1500 MBA x 48 months

Monthly Benefit Amount	$1500
Monthly payments between age 62 and FRA	x48
Total Social Security payable before FRA	$72,000

To calculate at what point you begin to lose the advantage of taking the benefit at age 62:

Total paid between age 62 and age 66 = $72,000. Divide $72,000 by the $500 monthly benefit lost by taking the benefit early - $72,000/$500 = 144 months. This means that after 144 months or 12 years (at age 74), you would begin to realize the <u>disadvantage</u> of having taking benefits at age 62.

Anyone who chooses to delay taking their Retirement Benefits until age 70 will see a significant increase in their permanent monthly benefit. For each month beyond a person's full retirement age, the benefits can increase by 2/3 of 1% for Delayed Retirement Credits (DRC).

Scenario 2 - Comparing benefits at Age 66 (FRA) to Age 70 with (DRCs)

Primary Insurance Amount at FRA (age 66) $2000
Four years of DRCs at 8% per year (age 70)   x32%
Realize a gain of $640 per month by waiting until age 70 $ 640
Add the DRC increase of $640 per month to the $2000 PIA = $2640 monthly benefit at age 70

To calculate the advantage of starting your benefit at age 66, multiply $2000 MBA x 48 months:

Monthly benefit at age 66 (FRA) $2000
Number of monthly payments between 66 and age 70   x48
Total Social Security payable before age 70 $96,000

To calculate at what point you begin to lose the advantage of starting the benefit at FRA:

Total payable before age 70 $96,000   150
Divided by the $640 (loss of DRCs) $640   =   12   = 12.5 years
You would be ahead for 150 months
150 months divided by 12 months = 12.5 years

You basically are trading an increase of $640 for life beginning at age 70 to receive $96,000 between age 66 and age 70. Obviously, $96,000 is a lot of money that you can put in your bank account before you are age 70. The decision to take your benefits at 62 versus your full retirement age or age 70 is one you will have to make. Consider your tax liability and other options to help you make the decision. Some people seek counsel from a trusted financial advisor or accountant or even a family member.

This calculation would look different for somebody whose full retirement age is beyond age 66. Someone whose FRA is 66 could have a maximum of 48 months (up to a 32% increase) while someone whose FRA is 67 could have a maximum of 36 months (up to a 24% increase).

If a Primary Insurance Amount is increased by Delayed Retirement Credits, that increased amount will be the amount used to calculate a survivor's benefits.

As noted above, if you are eligible for Spouse's Benefits, Widow(er)'s Benefit, or Surviving Divorced Spouse's Benefits, *see Chapters 3, 4, and 5.* If you have an option to take one type of benefit and save the other until your full retirement age or age 70, calculate the differences to determine the best choice for you. There are online calculators at **www.socialsecurity.gov/planners** to help you. You may also make an appointment with Social Security to discuss your options.

Earnings Test

(Working While Receiving Benefits)

It is true, you can receive Social Security benefits and still work. There are rules, however, that limit the amount you may earn without it affecting the benefits you are paid. Once you have reached your full retirement age, your earnings will no longer count against you. For your full retirement age, *see Tables 1 and 2, p. 58*. ***If you are receiving Social Security Disability Benefits or Supplemental Security Income Benefits, the rules for work and earnings are very different.*** *See Chapter 7, pp. 29-33, "SSI Benefits;" & Chapter 8, pp. 34-55, "Disability Benefits."*

Earnings are defined as remuneration for work performed for an employer or net self-employment income. **Income from investments, pensions, etc. are not counted as earnings**. Social Security refers to the amount of earnings allowed while working as the "Earnings Test." There is an <u>Annual Earnings Test</u> and a <u>Monthly Earnings Test</u>. The monthly earnings test is $1/12^{th}$ of the annual amount allowed. Generally, you may use the Monthly Earnings Test only one time. The earnings amount allowed for the year usually increases annually. Earnings Test changes for the following year are announced at the end of each calendar year. The amounts used in the examples to follow are for 2018. *See pp. 62-64, "Earnings Test Examples."*

The earnings amount allowed for the year in which you reach your full retirement age is much higher. See Table 3 below. *See Tables 1 & 2, p. 58, to determine your Full Retirement Age (FRA).*

Table 3

Working While Receiving Benefits (2018 and 2019 Amounts)	
If under Full Retirement Age (FRA), you are allowed to earn $17,040 in gross earnings for <u>2018</u> without benefits being affected. That increases to gross earnings of $17,640 in <u>2019</u>.	Social Security will withhold from your benefits $1 for every $2 you earn above the limit.
The Earnings Test is higher in the year you reach FRA. In <u>2018</u>, gross earnings can be $45,360 for months up to your FRA. Gross earnings increases to $46,920 before FRA for <u>2019.</u>	Social Security will withhold from your benefits $1 for every $3 you earn over the limit until the month in which you reach your FRA.
At FRA or older, there is no limit on earnings.	There is no offset against benefits.

Each year Social Security reviews the benefit records of all recipients who continue to work. If your earnings for the prior year can increase your benefit, Social Security will make the change and notify you by mail of what the increase will be. This is called a *"Recomputation" of your benefit (Primary Insurance Amount) and is done automatically.* A recomputation increases your benefit effective with January of the current year. You will then receive a one-time deposit to your bank account for months retroactive to January and the permanent increase will be applied to your ongoing monthly benefit. It can take six to nine months before it is done.

Earnings Test Examples

Example 1
***Annual* Earnings Test – If <u>under</u> Full Retirement Age (FRA) and working.**
Jane turned age 62 on January 2, 2018. She wants to start her benefits as soon as possible because she switched to part-time work. She expects to earn about $20,920 for the year. The 2018 Annual Earnings Test for someone under full retirement age is $17,040. A calculation must be done to determine if she can receive benefits in 2018 based on her earnings. Her monthly benefit amount payable at age 62 is $1000. This means Jane is eligible for $12,000 in 2018 (12 months x $1000). Since she is earning over the Annual Earnings Test Limit of $17,040, a calculation must be done to determine how the excess earnings will affect her.

Jane's estimated earnings	$20,920
Minus earnings amount allowed for 2018	17,040
Excess earnings	$3,880

Only $1 of every $2 over $17,040 affects the benefits payable to her in 2018. *See Table 3, p. 61.*

The excess of $3,880 is divided by 2. This results in $1940 that must be held back before benefits can be paid to Jane.

Jane's full Social Security benefits for January and February of 2018 ($2000 total) will be withheld to offset the $1940 in excess earnings. The $60 difference will be paid to Jane in 2019 after her 2018 earnings are verified by the Internal Revenue Service.

Benefits due Jane in 2018 would look very different if she were to reach full retirement age in 2018. She would receive all 12 months of benefits because her total estimated earnings would not exceed the Annual Earnings Test amount of $45,360 for 2018. *See Table 3, p. 61.*

If you start your Retirement Benefits early and subsequently have some months before full retirement age that you do not receive a full Social Security benefit, an adjustment will be made in your benefit. This adjustment is done after you reach your full retirement age. It is called an Adjusted Reduction Factor (ARF). Because the percentage of reduction is based on the month you start your benefits, it must be adjusted if you do not receive a benefit for all months before your full retirement age. This occurs due to work and earnings which result in benefits withheld. See below.

When you review Example 1 above, you will see that Jane's benefit, at the time of her filing, was reduced for 48 months (because she is taking her benefits at 62 instead of 66). At age 66, when Social Security reviews Jane's benefit record, the reduction will change to show that she should have only 46 months of reduction. Because of excess earnings, Jane did not get the first two months of benefits in 2018. Social Security will send her a notice once the ARF action is taken to inform her of the increase in her benefit.

Example 2
Monthly **Earnings Test – if under Full Retirement Age (FRA) and working.**
Because many people like to retire during the year instead of waiting until the end of the year, Social Security allows the **one-time** use of a monthly retirement test. It is usually the year in which one retires. It allows you to receive benefits for any month in which you have earnings under the monthly limit. In 2018, the monthly limit is $1420 (which is 1/12 of the $17,040 annual limit).

Charlotte, age 62 effective January 2018, files for benefits the same month. She will be eligible for a reduced benefit of $1000 per month which would total $12,000 for the year. She expects to earn $30,000 for months January through March. She will go part-time in April and plans to keep her earnings at $1300 per month April through December (which will total $11,700).

Charlotte's full-time earnings for Jan – March	$30,000
Her part-time earnings for April – Dec	+11,700
Total earnings too high to pay benefits	$41,700 (based on Annual Retirement Test)
Charlotte's total earnings	$41,700
Minus Annual Earnings Test amount	-17,040
Excess earnings	$24,660
Excess earnings	$24,660 divided by 2 = $12,330

Before benefits could be paid to Charlotte based on the Annual Retirement test, Social Security would have to hold back $12,330 in benefits. Charlotte is due only $12,000 in benefits for the year, thus she would not be entitled to benefits in 2018.

However, Charlotte can use the **one-time** **Monthly Retirement Test** which means she can receive a benefit for any month that she has earnings under $1,420 (1/12 of $17,040 – the Annual Retirement Test amount for 2018).

Charlotte would receive 9 months of benefits (April through December 2018) at $1000 per month for a total of $9,000 in 2018. She can do this only one year. Beginning in 2019, her benefits payable would be subject to the Annual Retirement test limit. After she reaches her full retirement age, earnings will have no effect on the payment of her Social Security benefits.

Example 3
Annual **Earnings Test – for work in year of Full Retirement Age (FRA).**
In January 2018, Ralph files for Social Security benefits to be effective with January 2018. He stated he earns $10,000 per month and had no plans to retire, thus his 2018 earnings would total $120,000. He is due $2700 per month in Social Security benefits and wants to use the money to help with his son's college education.

Because Ralph reaches his full retirement age in May 2018, he could earn up to $45,360 for the months before his full retirement age. Since Ralph plans to earn only $40,000 for the four months before he turns age 66, he is entitled to benefits for all 12 months in 2018.

Important: A maximum of six months of benefits can be paid retroactively, and only if you are at least six months past your full retirement age. For example, if Ralph reaches his full retirement age of 66 in May 2017 waited until June 2018 to file for his benefits, he could choose to receive benefits back to December 2017. He would get a retroactive benefit payment for that six-month period.

Note: If this were his situation, he would also earn Delayed Retirement Credits of 2/3 of 1% for each month between May 2017 (his full retirement age) and November 2017.

You may check your options and get estimates of benefits by using Social Security's online calculators at **www.socialsecurity.gov/planners.** If you still have questions about your options, you may call Social Security at 1-800-772-1213 (TTY-1-800-325-0778). However, Social Security employees are not to advise you of what you should do. They can simply answer your questions about your options.

Retirement vs Survivor Benefit Calculation

If you are simultaneously eligible for two or more types of benefits, such as your own Retirement Benefit, a Widow(er)'s Benefit, or a Divorced Spouse's Benefit, consider your options. Children may also receive survivor benefits. *See p. 69, "Child's Benefit Calculation."*

Example

David was preparing to file for his own Retirement Benefit at age 66 when his wife, Ruth, died. His Primary Insurance Amount (PIA) is $2200 per month. Ruth had a PIA of $1800 per month. She was not receiving benefits at the time of her death. This means Ruth's full PIA of $1800 is payable to David. David has options. He can file for his own and receive $2200 per month or he can file as a widower on his wife's record and receive $1800 per month. At first glance, one thinks filing for the higher benefit on his own record would be more advantageous. Consider the following:

David could file for his own benefit at $2200 per month. That would be his lifetime benefit (except for cost of living increases) or,

David could file for the Widower's Benefit at $1800 per month and allow his PIA of $2200 to earn Delayed Retirement Credits of 8% per year until he is age 70. That would result in a 32% increase of $704 on his own benefit and make him eligible for $2904 per month for the rest of his life beginning at age 70.

To compare the options above, calculate what he is due on his own record between the time he starts his benefit until age 70 - $2200 x 48 months = $105,600. Compare that amount to what he would be due as a widower for the same time period - $1800 x 48 months = $86,400.

The difference is $19,200. That is what he would lose for the four years between age 66 and age 70 by taking the Widower's Benefit. If David takes his own benefit at age 66 rather than age 70, he is basically trading an additional $704 per month for the rest of his life (beginning at age 70) to receive $19,200 more in benefits between age 66 and age 70.

Divide the $19,200 by the $704. The advantage of taking his own benefit at age 66 would be lost within 27 months.

Clearly, it seems the better option for David is to take the lower benefit at age 66 and save his own until he is age 70. However, David must make that decision. There might be reasons why he wants to take his own higher benefit at age 66.

Be aware of possible options. Calculate the differences on www.socialsecurity.gov/planners. You may also contact the Social Security Administration to ask for assistance. Social Security personnel cannot advise you what to do but they can help you understand your options.

Spouse and Divorced Spouse Benefit Calculation

Example

In July of 2018, Bill filed for unreduced Retirement Benefits. Bill's date of birth is July 5, 1952. His full retirement age is 66. He filed for his benefits to be effective July 2018. He indicated on his application that he has a spouse, Nancy, who was born April 12, 1953. She started receiving her own benefits at age 64 in April of 2017. To determine her eligibility as a spouse, the following calculation would be done.

Compare Nancy's unreduced benefit, Primary Insurance Amount (PIA), of $980 to 50% of Bill's unreduced benefit, (PIA), of $2400. Since Nancy's PIA does not exceed 50% of Bill's PIA of $1200, Nancy is due a Spouse's Benefit.

Nancy's $980 PIA reduced for 24 months (5/9 of 1% x 24) results in a $130 reduction in her PIA. This results in a monthly benefit of $850. To calculate her Spouse's Benefits, you compare the unreduced amounts, then reduce the difference to determine the Spouse's Benefit.

Potential Spouse's Benefit on Bill's record	$1200
Nancy's own unreduced benefit (PIA)	-980
Nancy's Spouse's Benefit at her FRA	$ 220

The $220 difference must be reduced for the number of months that Nancy receives Spouse's Benefits before her full retirement age. The Spouse's Benefit has a different reduction factor per month. The reduction factor for a Spouse's Benefit is 25/36 of 1% for the first 36 months and 5/12 of 1% for each additional month before full retirement age.

The $220 is reduced for the nine months between July 2018 and April 2019 (25/36 of 1% x 9) results in a $13 reduction. The $207 difference is added to Nancy's own reduced benefit of $850.

Nancy's own reduced benefit	$ 850
Her reduced Spouse's Benefit	+207
Total monthly benefit starting July 2018	$1057

Note: Since Bill was born before January 2, 1954, he could consider filing a Restricted Application for Spouse's Benefits on Nancy's record delaying his own until age 70 to earn Delayed Retirement Credits. *See pp. 67-68, "Restricted Application Calculation."*

Additionally: If you are filing as a divorced spouse and had two or more previous marriages that meet the requirements for a Divorced Spouse's Benefit, ask Social Security to help you understand what your options are. You might be able to file on one record at age 62 and the other at your full retirement age to receive a higher lifetime benefit. Also, if you were born before January 2, 1954, *see pp. 67-68, "Restricted Application Calculation;" & Chapter 4, pp. 15-19, "Divorced Spouse's Benefits."*

A Divorced Spouse's Benefit is calculated using the same formula that is used for a spouse. However, the Divorced Spouse's Benefit does not affect the total benefits payable to the family. *See p. 70, "Family Maximum Calculation."*

Restricted Application Calculation

People born before January 2, 1954, who are full retirement age may delay taking their own benefit until full retirement age or age 70, and file for benefits on a spouse's or divorced spouse's record. The spouse on whose record the application is filed must be receiving benefits. For details on how to qualify for Spouse's Benefits or Divorced Spouse's Benefits, *see Chapter 3, pp. 10-14, "Spouse's Benefits;" or Chapter 4, pp. 15-19, "Divorced Spouse's Benefits."*

Example

Maude – Born on October 02, 1952, turned age 66 on October 2, 2018. Maude did not want to file for benefits until she reached her full retirement age (66 for her).

Maude's husband, Clyde is already receiving his Social Security benefits. Maude learned that since she was born before January 2, 1954, she has an option. She can file as a spouse at her full retirement age on her husband's record and delay application for her own Retirement Benefit until she turns age 70. This would allow her to receive a much higher benefit at age 70 by earning Delayed Retirement Credits of 8% per year between age 66 and age 70.

To determine what would be more advantageous, the following computation would be done:

1st – Determine what Maude's Primary Insurance Amount would be on her own record at age 66 - $1700 per month.

2nd – Determine what Maude would be due on her husband's record at her age 66. His Primary Insurance Amount (PIA) is $2000. Her Spouse's Benefit can be up to 50% of her husband's PIA. Since she could start receiving Spouse's Benefits at her age 66, she would be due $1000 per month.

3rd – Calculate how much Maude could receive between age 66 and 70 (48 months) on her record $1700 x 48 months = $81,600.

4th – Calculate how much Maude could receive between age 66 and 70 as a spouse on her husband's record $1,000 x 48 months = $48,000. Note, if she chose to take benefits on her own record, she would not be eligible for a Spouse's Benefit. Her own benefit of $1700 exceeds 50% ($1,000) of her husband's benefit of $2,000.

5th – Subtract what she could receive as a spouse for 48 months from what she could receive on her own for 48 months - $81,600 minus $48,000 = $33,600. The $33,600 is the total amount of money she would lose for that four-year period by taking the Spouse's Benefit instead of her own.

6th – Multiply what her own benefit could be if she waits until age 70 to earn Delayed Retirement Credits of 32% on top of her $1700. That adds up to $2,244 per month instead of $1700.

Comparing her options:

Benefits on her own at 66	$1700
Number of months before 70	x48
Total Payable	$81,600

Benefits due as a spouse at 66 $1000
Number of months before 70   x48
Total Payable $48,000

Maude has to decide if she wants to file for the Spouse's Benefit and save her own until she is age 70. To wait until age 70 to start her own benefit, would mean that her $1700 Primary Insurance Amount would be increased 32% due to Delayed Retirement Credits of 8% per year. Her total lifetime benefit (except for cost of living adjustments) would be $2244 which is $544 more per month than the $1700 she is due at her full retirement age.

To compare her options, subtract the difference between what she could receive on her own before age 70 versus what she would receive as a spouse for the same period.

Her own (between age 66 and 70) $81,600
Her Spouse's Benefit (between age 66 and 70)   - 48,000
Difference $33,600

The $33,600 she would be losing for 48 months is then divided by what she would be giving up for the rest of her life if she waited until age 70. That amount is the extra $544.

$33,600 divided by $544 = 61.76 months or 5.14 years. The advantage of taking her own benefit at her FRA would be lost in less than 6 years.

If you are simultaneously eligible for two or more types of benefits, it pays to understand your options. For example, if longevity runs in Maude's family and she were to live until age 80, she would receive $65,280 (120 months x $544) more in benefits between her 70th and 80th birthday by saving her own until she is age 70. If she were to live another 10 years, (to age 90) that amount would double to $130,560.

You may calculate the benefit amounts and compare your options by using Social Security's online calculators at **www.socialsecurity.gov/planners.** You may also call Social Security's 800# service to ask for assistance. Social Security employees can help you understand your options. They are not allowed to advise you of what to do.

Child's Benefit Calculation

Social Security benefits for eligible children are determined by the type of benefit to be paid on the wage earner's record (retirement, disability, or survivor benefits), the wage earner's Primary Insurance Amount(PIA) and Family Maximum allowed on the record. The amounts in the example below are based on 2018 bend points. *See Chapter 9, p. 70, "Family Maximum Calculation."*

If the benefit being paid is on a retirement or disability record, the child's benefit cannot exceed 50% of the PIA. If it is a survivor benefit, the child's benefit cannot exceed 75% of the PIA.

Example

Jack is starting his Social Security Retirement Benefits at his full retirement age of 66. He has a wife and three sons who will qualify on his record. His sons' ages are 17, 16, and 12. Jack's wife is 48. She is due benefits because they have a child under age 16.

Jack's Primary Insurance Amount is $2000. The Family Maximum amount is $3562. Jack will receive $2000 per month. The difference between his PIA and the Family Maximum is $1562. The three children plus his wife must share that amount. Each of the four family members will receive $390 (rounded down).

When the 17-year old son turns age 18 and is no longer in high school, his eligibility ends and the Family Maximum of $1562 will allow benefits for the other three family members to increase to $520 each.

The monthly benefit will change again when the 16-year old son is no longer eligible. At that time, the $1562 will be divided by two family members. The youngest son who is still eligible and his mother will each receive $781 per month.

When the youngest son turns age 16, the mother can no longer receive benefits unless she is at least age 62. The benefit for the last child on the record increases to $1000. It cannot exceed 50% of Jack's PIA.

When the wife turns age 62, she can file on the record as a spouse. Her benefit can be no more than 50% of Jack's PIA which would be $1000. She would then be reduced by approximately 37.5% for taking the benefit at age 62. If she is eligible on her own work record, that benefit would have to be calculated before a Spouse's Benefit could be considered. And, if the spouse is working, earnings would have to be considered. *See Chapter 9, p. 61, "Earnings Test;" Chapter 9, pp. 62-64, "Earnings Test Examples;" Chapter 3, pp. 10-14, "Spouse's Benefits," & Chapter 4, pp. 15-19, "Divorced Spouse's Benefits."*

If Jack were deceased, the benefits to be paid would increase to 75% of Jack's PIA. If his widow and three children were eligible, the total Family Maximum of $3562 would be divided among four family members.

A divorced spouse (if eligible) can receive on the same record without it affecting the other family members. The Divorced Spouse's Benefit is not included in the Family Maximum.

Family Maximum Calculation

There is a maximum benefit amount that can be paid on any Social Security benefit record. There are set formulas for determining the maximum family benefit. Generally, the maximum on the retirement/survivor record falls between 150% to 188% of the Primary Insurance Amount (PIA) on the record. See formula details at **www.socialsecurity.gov/OACT/COLA/familymax.html.**

Family members are due up to 50% of the PIA on a life record (wage earner is receiving Retirement Benefits or Disability Benefits). The total family benefits cannot exceed the Family Maximum.

For example, if the PIA on a living wage earner's record is $1000 and the Family Maximum is $1500, the wage earner could receive $1000 at full retirement age. One eligible family member could be entitled up to $500 per month. If there are more family members eligible, the $500 would be divided proportionately. **The wage earner's own benefit is never affected by the Family Maximum.** Additionally, benefits paid to a divorced spouse or surviving divorced have no affect on other family benefits, e.g. spouse and/or children.

On a survivor record, family members are eligible for 75% of the PIA, not to exceed the Family Maximum. Using the same example from above with the deceased wage earner having a PIA of $1000 and a Family Maximum of $1500, up to two family members could receive $750 each. This equals 75% of the PIA ($1000) and does not exceed the Family Maximum ($1500). If there are other family members eligible, the $1500 would be divided by the total number of eligible dependents. For example, if there is a widow and three young children in her care, each one would receive $375.

On a disability record, the Family Maximum formula differs based on many factors. Sometimes, the Family Maximum is the same as the disabled wage earner's PIA which means there are no benefits payable to anyone other than the disabled wage earner. These formulas are all built into the online calculators which you may use to query what benefits might be due you and your family should you become disabled. You may also call Social Security's 800# service to ask what the Family Maximum would be if you were to file for Disability Benefits.

Even if the Family Maximum for Disability Benefits is the same as the PIA, you are advised to file for family members. It could protect your family should anything change on your record in the future. Social Security calls this an application for "technical benefits."

To complicate things further, there is a formula for a *combined* Family Maximum. This occurs when there is a child due on two different Social Security benefit records on which other eligible children can be paid. This is very complex and would be addressed if and when it occurs (which is rare).

The Appeals Process

If you file an application for Social Security benefits, you will receive a letter from the Social Security Administration informing you of the decision on your claim. If your claim for benefits is approved, your letter will explain the type of benefit to be received, when the benefit will start (or should have started), and how much the monthly benefit will be. If you are due benefits for a retroactive period, the letter should state the amount of retroactive benefits due and identify the retroactive months for which they are being paid. Sometimes, your benefits will be deposited to your bank account before you receive your letter. The letter also lists your reporting responsibilities, i.e., what changes should be reported, such as changes in work, marital status, address, or direct deposit information.

The letter includes instructions on how to file an appeal and what type of appeal to file if your claim is denied or if you disagree with some part of the decision on your approved claim (i.e., when your benefits should start). It informs you that you have 60 days in which to file the appeal. If you do not file it within 60 days, you are agreeing with the decision issued on your claim. The Social Security Administration presumes you received the letter within five days of the notice date on the letter.

There are three different appeals that can be filed with the Social Security Administration. Beyond that, if a person is still not satisfied with the Social Security Administration's decision, the next step is a civil suit. Most appeals can be filed online. Filing online usually results in a quicker decision.
- The first appeal is called a Reconsideration (*Form SSA-561* or *i561* if filing online).
- The second appeal is called a Hearing (*Form SSA-501* or *i501* if filing online).
- The third appeal is called an Appeals Council Review *(Form HA-520)*. At this time, an Appeals Council Review cannot be requested online. You must do a paper form HA-520.

You may call the Social Security Administration at 1-800-772-1213 (TTY 1-800-325-0778) to request paper forms or you may do an online form if filing a Reconsideration or Hearing at www.socialsecurity.gov. Select "Search" feature and type in "Appeal a Decision."

Reconsideration
A Reconsideration is usually the first step in the appeals process. You may submit the *Form SSA-561,* or complete the online *Form i561*, or you may write a letter asking for a review of the decision on your claim. It must be submitted to the agency within 60 days of the receipt of your notice. The 60-day period begins five days after the notice date on your letter. If filing a medical appeal, you must submit the *Form SSA-3441* (medical questionnaire) and *Form SSA-827* (authorization to get medical reports) at the same time.
Note: Some states have eliminated the Reconsideration step and allow the applicant to file a Hearing as their first appeal. Currently, those states are Alabama, Alaska, Colorado, Louisiana, Michigan, Missouri, New Hampshire, New York, Pennsylvania and some parts of California. *Your denial letter from the Social Security Administration will advise you of which appeal you should file.*

Be prepared to provide evidence of why you think the Social Security Administration decision is wrong. The evidence required will vary depending on the type of application you filed. Most appeals are filed on disability applications. Some disability claims are denied because not all medical evidence was submitted. You should review your disability decision letter from the Social Security Administration to determine what medical records were used for the decision. If you see that some medical information is not listed, you can call the Social Security Administration to ask to review the file. This will help you determine what information you should try to obtain to support your Reconsideration request.

It is difficult to know how long it will take to get a decision on your Reconsideration. Again, depending on what type of decision you are appealing, such as a benefit amount versus a medical decision, it could take as little as 30 days or as long as 6 months, but on average, it is 2 to 3 months.

The Social Security Administration will notify you by mail of the decision made on your Reconsideration request. If you are not satisfied with that decision, you will be informed of your right to file for a Hearing.

Hearing
The second appeal level is a Hearing, unless you live in a state that skips the Reconsideration appeal. Currently, if you live in Alabama, Alaska, Colorado, Louisiana, Michigan, Missouri, New Hampshire, New York, Pennsylvania and some parts of California, the Hearing is your first appeal level. Your denial letter from the Social Security Administration will advise you which appeal to file. In either case, you have 60 days in which to file your Hearing. The 60-day period begins five days after the notice date on your letter. You can file a Hearing by completing the *Form SSA-501* or online Form *i501*. A Hearing allows you to appear in person or by videoconferencing before an Administrative Law Judge (ALJ). An ALJ is a lawyer trained in Social Security law and regulations. At the Hearing, you can give testimony to why you disagree with the Social Security Administration's decision on your claim and/or you can appoint somebody to represent you and speak for you. The ALJ might also ask you questions about your claim to get more clarification on the issues involved.

When you file your request, the paperwork is mailed or electronically transferred to a Hearing Office. Your Hearing request is added to a roster and is tracked electronically until the decision is rendered. This decision can take several months and sometimes up to two years depending on the backlogs. The Hearing office must be able to schedule an ALJ to hear your case. The ALJ tries to hold your Hearing at a location within 75 miles of your address. Many Social Security offices are set up with extra space to permit Hearings on site. You are likely to be scheduled sooner if you agree to a Hearing by videoconference. You would be notified of the date and location for the videoconference. A technician is on site to assist with the setup. You will be able to see the ALJ and he/she will be able to see and speak with you via video. You may also request to not appear. However, it is usually in your best interest to appear in person or by videoconferencing or to have a representative appear for you.

Many people feel ill-prepared to handle some of the complexities involved in proving their case. If you want someone to represent you, you must sign an authorization *Form SSA-1696-U4, Appointment of Representative*. If the representative is not an attorney, he/she must also sign the form. You are not required to have a representative at the Hearing. However, if you choose to have a representative, be sure it is someone knowledgeable about Social Security law. Ask about their experience with Social Security claims. The representative's role is to act on your behalf, assist in getting information needed to support your claim (such as medical reports for a disability claim). Not all attorneys know Social Security law. The Social Security Administration field office can sometimes provide you with a list of names of attorneys or other firms dedicated to representing claimants in the Social Security appeals process. The Social Security Administration cannot, however, recommend any particular person or firm.

Should you appoint a representative whom you agree to pay, that representative or a Social Security Claims Specialist can advise you what form(s) you will need to sign. Be aware that the representative can charge you up to 25% of retroactive benefits (not to exceed $6000) if you are approved. That fee must be approved by the Social Security Administration before it can be paid. A representative handling your appeal must file your medical appeal online if he/she wants Social Security to pay the fees directly to them.

You may appoint someone you know, a firm, or an attorney to represent you at any appeal level. It is rarely done for the first appeal level (Reconsideration); frequently done for the second appeal (Hearing); and sometimes done for the third appeal level (Appeals Council Review).

When the Hearing decision is made, you will be mailed a letter from the Social Security Administration. This could be in as few as 6 months or as many as 24 months or longer. If your Hearing is approved, you'll be notified of the retroactive benefits you are due. If you had a representative who will be requesting fee reimbursement, you'll be notified of the amount that will be withheld from your retroactive benefits. If you are denied, you will be advised that you can file for an Appeals Council Review (From HA-520).

Appeals Council Review

This is the third appeals level. If you disagree with the decision made on your Hearing, you may ask to have it reviewed by the Appeals Council. You make your request known by completing the form *Request for Review of Hearing Decision/Order (HA-520)*. Currently, you must submit a paper form for this review. It cannot be done online. If the Appeals Council supports a finding for a review, it can decide on your case or return it to the Administrative Law Judge for further review.

If the Appeals Council agrees with the Hearing decision and you are not satisfied with that decision, your next step would be to file a lawsuit in a federal district court within the required time frame. Your notice from Social Security will provide instructions on how to do this.

Medicare
Medicare Eligibility
Requirements
- Be a U.S citizen, or an alien lawfully admitted for permanent residence and have resided in the U.S. for five consecutive years prior to enrollment in Medicare, and
- Be eligible for Social Security Retirement, Disability, Spouse's, Divorced Spouse's, Widow(er)'s, Surviving Divorced Spouse's Benefits, or be certified as eligible for Railroad Board Benefits
- **And** any one of the following:

Age 65 or older	**Be entitled to at least 24 months of Social Security Disability Benefits**
End State Renal Disease (ESRD)	**Diagnosed with Amyotrophic Lateral Sclerosis (ALS) (aka Lou Gehrig's disease)**

Four Parts of Medicare
- Part A - Hospital Insurance
- Part B - Medical Insurance
- Part C - Medicare Advantage Plan, aka Medicare Managed Plan
- Part D - Medicare Prescription Drug Plan

Part A (Hospital Insurance) Coverage
o Inpatient care
o Skilled nursing facility care
o Hospice care
o Home health care

Part B (Medical Insurance) Coverage
o Doctors who treat you in or out of the hospital
o Emergency Room Services
o Laboratory Work
o Cancer Screenings
o Chemotherapy
o Durable Medical Equipment
o Cardiac Rehabilitation
o Physical Therapy
o Glaucoma Tests
o Depression Screening
o Flu Shots

- o Hepatitis B Shots
- o Kidney Dialysis and Supplies
- o Diabetes Supplies
- o HIV Screening
- o STD Screening
- o Chiropractic Services
- o Mammograms
- o PSA exams (prostate cancer)
- o Yearly Wellness Visit
- o Many other services (Check your *Medicare & You* handbook or www.Medicare.gov)

Part C (Medicare Advantage Plan)

- Private health insurance plans run by Medicare-approved insurance companies
- Includes benefits and services covered under Part A and Part B of Medicare
- Some plans include Medicare prescription drug coverage. If so, a Part D plan is not needed. Some plans also offer dental and vision coverage

Part D (Medicare Prescription Drug Plan)

- Medicare-contracted plans offered by private insurance companies
- Plans help cover the cost of prescription drugs

Every person who becomes entitled to Medicare will receive in the mail a *Medicare & You* handbook. Please take time to read the Table of Contents. This will alert you to information that is pertinent to you. Each year a new handbook is issued. You may also access the handbook online through www.Medicare.gov.

Note: The Social Security Administration does not administer the Medicare program. Social Security enrolls eligible individuals in the program. Once you are enrolled in Medicare, questions regarding your health care benefits should be directed to Centers for Medicare and Medicaid Services (CMS) 1-800-633-4227 (TTY 1-877-486-2048). You may check the CMS website for information at www.Medicare.gov. You should also consider setting up your personal Medicare account at www.mymedicare.gov. This will allow you to review your Medicare record online. *See Chapter 1, pp. 4, "Contacting Medicare."*

Part A Medicare Costs for 2019

If you are eligible for Social Security or Railroad benefits, you will have no monthly premium for Part A. If you have only 30 to 39 Social Security work credits, you will pay a premium of $240.00 per month. If you have fewer than 30 work credits, your premium will be $437.00 per month. If you have End Stage Renal Disease and do not have the required credits listed above, contact Social Security to determine if you qualify for Medicare based on special rules.

Hospital Care Deductibles and Copays

To qualify, you must be admitted as an *inpatient* for an overnight stay by doctor's orders. Overnight Observation Care is not covered under Medicare Part A.

Hospital Inpatient Costs

$1364   deductible during each **60-day benefit period**. *A benefit period begins with the day of admission and ends 60 days after you are discharged.* If you are hospitalized again beyond the 60-day benefit period, you will have to pay another deductible.

$341   per day for days 61-90

$682   per day for days 91-150 (Lifetime Reserve – one-time use only)

Skilled Nursing Care

To qualify, your doctor must certify that you need daily skilled care or physical therapy following a three-day hospital stay. Care must be skilled nursing care, not custodial care.

Skilled Nursing Care Costs for each benefit period (see above)

No cost   first 20 days

$170.50   days 21-100

100%   after day 100

Hospice Care

To qualify, a Hospice doctor must certify that you are terminally ill and have a life expectancy of less than six months. If approved by Medicare, you may receive care in your home or other facility such as a nursing home.

Other services covered as follows:

- Medical and nursing care
- Certain durable medical equipment
- Items and services needed for pain relief

Hospice Care Costs

No costs if certain requirements are met

$5   copay for some outpatient prescription drugs

5%   of Medicare-approved amount for inpatient respite care

Home Health Care

To qualify, your care must be certified by a physician.

Home Health Care Costs

$0   for home health care services

20%   of the Medicare-approved amount for durable medical equipment

Part B Medicare Costs for 2019

Your Part B Cost in 2019
$135.50 Monthly Premium (or higher based on income – see Table 1 below)
$185.00 Annual Deductible
Coinsurance - You pay 20% of Medicare's "reasonable charge" after deductible met

If you do not sign up for Part B when first eligible, and you do not meet the rules for a Special Enrollment Period (SEP), you will be charged a 10% penalty for each 12-month period that you could have had Medicare Part B but did not take it.

Your Part B premiums could be higher than the standard monthly premium if your Modified Adjusted Gross Income (MAGI), as reported on your tax returns from two years earlier, falls within the guidelines below.

Part B Medicare premiums based on your MAGI from two years ago (as shown on your IRS tax return). See table below.

Income-Related Monthly Adjustment Amount (IRMAA)

Using 2017 Annual Income			2019 Part B Monthly Premium
Single Individual	Married Filing Joint Tax Return	Married Filing Individual Tax Return	
$85,000 or less	$170,000 or less	$85,000 or less	$135.50
$85,001 - $107,000	$170,001 - $214,000	N/A	$189.60
$107,001 - $133,500	$214,001 - $267,000	N/A	$270.90
$133,501 - $160,000	$267,001 - $320,000	N/A	$352.20
$160,001 - $500,000	$320,001 - $750,000	Above $85,000 and less than $415,000	$433.40
$500,001 or above	$750,001 and above	$415,000 and above	$460.50

Income-Related Monthly Adjustment Amount (IRMAA)
If you experience a life changing event that could reduce your premium surcharge, you may submit a request to Social Security, or to the Railroad Board if you are a railroad retiree. Some life-changing events are loss of wages or other income, divorce, remarriage, and death of spouse. Access *Form SSA-44* (Medicare Income-Related Monthly Adjustment Amount, Life - Changing Event) at https://www.ssdfacts.com/forms/SSA-44.pdf. Download the form, complete it, and submit it with proof of the change to your local Social Security office or mail it to the Railroad Board. For further information, contact Social Security at 1-800-772-1213 (TTY 1-877-486-2048) or the Railroad Board at 1-877-772-5772 (TTY 1-312-751-4701).

Part A & B Enrollment

Part A Enrollment

Enrollment in Part A Hospital Insurance is automatic if you are already receiving benefits at the time you turn age 65 or after 24 months of Disability Benefits. Your Medicare card will be mailed to you showing effective dates for Parts A and Part B. If, however, you or your spouse are still working, and you are covered under an employer group health insurance plan, you should consider returning the Medicare card to have it reissued with Part A only. See "Part B Enrollment" below.

If you are turning age 65 and do not plan to file for benefits, you should contact Social Security three months before age 65 to file for Part A of Medicare. You may file online for Medicare at www.socialsecurity.gov or call to make an appointment 1-800-772-1213 (TTY 1-800-325-0778).

Part B Enrollment

Some people question why they should pay for health insurance when they are healthy and feel they do not need it. They prefer to wait until they *need* it to buy it. But there are very specific enrollment guidelines. If you do not have an acceptable reason for not taking Part B of Medicare during the appropriate enrollment period, you can suffer a 10% penalty for each 12-month period beyond the time you should have enrolled. The penalty remains on the premium for a lifetime.

When you should delay enrolling in Part B

Questions to be answered by you:

- Are you still working, or do you have a spouse who is still working?
- Do you or your spouse have health insurance coverage as an active employee provided by the employer or union? COBRA is not considered an acceptable employer plan for Part B purposes.
- Does the employer have at least 20 employees? If you are receiving Medicare based on a disability, the employer must have at least 100 employees.
- Will you need to purchase a Supplemental Medicare Plan (Medigap) when you retire and/or lose your employer health insurance plan?

If you answered YES to all the above questions, you should consider refusing Part B of Medicare until you, or your spouse, no longer have an *active* employee status. A couple months before you or your spouse retire, you should contact Social Security to notify them that you or your spouse are retiring and losing your employer health insurance plan and that you need to be enrolled in Part B of Medicare. If you are not going to have a health insurance plan provided by your employer or union once you have retired, then you should consider enrolling in a Medigap plan within six months of your Part B start date. A Medigap plan covers the gaps in Medicare – such as the deductibles and copays that you must pay before Medicare pays anything. It is highly recommended that you purchase this extra coverage to avoid the possibility of high out-of-pocket costs should you suffer a serious medical issue. *See Chapter 12, pp. 92-96, "Supplemental Medical Insurance (Medigap)."*

If you (or your spouse) continue to work and are covered under a group health insurance plan, you should check with your employer to determine how that plan coordinates with Medicare.

Enrollment Periods - Overview

Please read this section very carefully. There are several factors that could result in problems with your Medicare start dates and premiums. *If you are penalized for not enrolling at the right time, the penalty is a lifetime charge.*

Even if you plan to continue working and have good health insurance through your employer or have a good health insurance plan from a spouse's active employment, you should consider filing for Part A Hospital Insurance <u>unless</u> your employer health insurance is a Health Savings Account (HSA). By signing up for Medicare while paying into your HSA, you lose your IRS tax advantage and can be penalized. This means you should not sign up for Social Security or Railroad benefits either. *By law, if you are receiving Social Security or Railroad benefits at age 65, Medicare Part A coverage takes effect. You cannot refuse it.*

There are several Medicare enrollment periods. Decide which one fits your situation.

- **Automatic Enrollment Period (AEP).** If you are already receiving Social Security or Railroad benefits when you turn age 65, your enrollment in Medicare Part A and B is automatic. Your Medicare card will be mailed to you, usually a month or so before you turn 65. You may refuse Part B of Medicare, but it needs to be for the right reason. *See p. 78, "Part B Enrollment."*

- **Initial Enrollment Period (IEP).** This is a 7-month period that begins 3 months before you are age 65, includes the month you turn age 65, and ends 3 months after you are age 65. If you sign up during the first 3 months of your IEP, your coverage for Part A and/or Part B starts the month you turn age 65. If you wait until the month you turn age 65 or during the following 3 months, your start date for Medicare will be delayed. Remember, if you were born on the 1st day of the month, you are deemed to have turned age 65 the month before. See IEP Table below.

Initial Enrollment Period (IEP) Table						
Month 1	Month 2	Month 3	Month of Age 65	Month 5	Month 6	Month 7
Coverage starts at age 65			Coverage starts 1st month after enrollment	Coverage starts 2nd month after enrollment	Coverage starts 3rd month after enrollment	

- **General Enrollment Period (GEP).** If you do not qualify for Medicare during an Automatic Enrollment Period and you miss your Initial Enrollment Period, you may enroll during the GEP, which is January 1- March 31 of each year. However, your coverage does not start until July 1st of that year. Also, you may have to pay a higher premium for your Part B of Medicare if it has been over 12 months since you were first eligible for Medicare.

- **Special Enrollment Period (SEP).** This allows protection for people who do not want to pay for Part B of Medicare while covered under an active employer group health insurance plan based on current work (their own or through a spouse). To qualify for this exception to regular

Part B enrollment, a person who is receiving retirement or survivor benefits must have coverage from an employer who has at least 20 employees. For a person receiving Disability Benefits, the employer must have at least 100 employees.

Note: There are occasions in which the Initial Enrollment Period and the Special Enrollment Period overlap. When that happens, the rules for the IEP apply. The SEP rules cannot apply until the IEP ends (see Table on page 79). Check with Social Security if you are not taking Part B of Medicare at age 65 but you plan to retire within three months after age 65 and will lose your health insurance under an active employer plan. Social Security can help you decide your options.

CAUTION: At the time of retirement and loss of the active employer's health insurance plan, enrollment in Medicare Part B must take place within eight months to avoid a penalty. Once Part B enrollment is effective, the six-month Medigap Guaranteed Issue Rights period begins. During this six-month period, a beneficiary may enroll in any Supplemental Medicare Plan (Medigap) without going through medical underwriting. *See Chapter 12, pp. 92-96, "Supplemental Medicare Insurance."*

Other Considerations

COBRA. People who elect COBRA after employment ends, have only 8 months to enroll in Part B even if COBRA lasts longer than 8 months. Once enrolled in Part B of Medicare, the six-month Open Enrollment Period for Medigap coverage begins. *See Chapter 12, pp. 92-96, "Supplemental Medical Insurance."*

End Stage Renal Disease (ESRD). You should sign up for Part A & B if/when diagnosed with ESRD. Medicare can cover three dialysis treatments per week, including laboratory tests, medications, home dialysis training, equipment, supplies and other services. Your dialysis facility will coordinate your care.

Railroad Beneficiaries. The Medicare program is the same as it is for Social Security beneficiaries. However, Railroad beneficiaries will have different contact sources. Contact the Railroad Board at 1-877-772-5772 (TTY 1-312-751-4701).

Residents of Puerto Rico. If you are receiving Social Security or Railroad benefits, Part A of Medicare starts automatically when you turn age 65 or after 24 months of Disability Benefits. However, you must sign up for Part B of Medicare. Social Security beneficiaries should contact your local field office or call Medicare at 1-800-633-4227 (TTY 1-877-486-2048). Railroad beneficiaries should call the Railroad Board at 1-877-772-5772 (TTY 1-312-751-4701).

Part B Coordination with Other Health Insurance

COBRA. Individuals covered under COBRA at the time they become eligible for Medicare should sign up for Medicare Part A & B to avoid a premium penalty for Part B. If the COBRA plan has a creditable prescription drug plan, they may delay signing up for Part D (Medicare prescription drug coverage) until the COBRA plan ends. Check with the COBRA carrier to verify if the drug plan is considered creditable for Medicare purposes.

Federal Retirees. Most federal retirees qualify for Medicare Part A & B. However, many federal employees refuse Part B because of the monthly premium. You might want to consider enrolling in Part B if it will result in 100% coverage of your health care needs. Once enrolled in Medicare, the federal employee health insurance becomes secondary and helps cover deductibles, and copays that Medicare does not cover. Retirees who refuse Part B when first eligible and then enroll at a later date, will be subject to the Part B penalty which lasts a lifetime.

Health Savings Accounts (HSA). If you have money left in a Health Savings Account after you become entitled to Medicare, you may use that money to help pay your Part B premiums, deductibles and copays. Once you are enrolled in Medicare, you risk having to pay IRS penalties if you continue to pay into a Health Savings Account. Contributions to your HSA should stop six months prior to filing for Medicare. If you are paying into a Health Savings Account and are within six months of age 65, talk with your employer regarding your options.

Marketplace or Private Insurance. Individuals insured through the Marketplace (under the Affordable Care Act) or other private insurance should take Part B of Medicare when they first become eligible. Check with your insurance carrier regarding possible exceptions.

Medicaid. Medicaid is a health insurance program for people with low income and limited resources. It is administered by your state and might have a different name in your state. Each state can determine the income and resource criteria differently, so check with your state agency to ask if you qualify. Do an online search for your state and county "Department of Social Services" or go to www.Medicare.gov/contacts to locate your local agency.

Medicare Savings Programs (MSP). Programs administered by your state Department of Social Services that can supplement your Medicare costs. To locate your agency, go to www.Medicare.gov/contacts.
- *QMB – Qualified Medicare Beneficiary.* QMB is a program in which your Part A premium (if not eligible based on credits) and Part B premium are paid for you. If you qualify, your deductible, coinsurance and copayment are also paid for you. Always show your Medicare and Medicaid card or QMB card when accessing health care.
- *SLMB – Special Low-Income Medicare Beneficiary.* SLMB is a program that helps pay the Part B premiums.
- *QI – Qualifying Individual.* QI is a program that also helps pay the Part B premium, but an application must be filed yearly.
- *QDWI – Qualified Disabled and Working Individuals.* QDWI helps pay Part A premiums only for Medicare beneficiaries who are disabled and working.
  Note: MSP programs are not offered in Puerto Rico or the Virgin Islands.

TRICARE. Military service members who qualify for TRICARE must also enroll in Part B when eligible unless covered as an active-duty service member, in which case, you may delay taking Part B (without penalty) until you retire.

Veterans. Veterans who use Veterans Administration services for all their health care needs can refuse Part B of Medicare but might want to consider taking Part B to have broader access to health care outside the VA facilities. Veterans who choose to enroll in Part B of Medicare at a later date will suffer the penalty for late enrollment. Additionally, veterans can consider enrollment in a Medigap plan at the same time they become eligible for Part B of Medicare.

In summary:

1st - Decide if you want to enroll in original Medicare, as outlined above, or enroll in a Medicare Advantage Plan (Medicare Part C). *See pp. 84-85, "Part C (Medicare Advantage Plans)."* Please read all the instructions regarding enrollment periods. *Failure to enroll timely could result in a lifetime penalty.*

2nd - You should consider enrolling in a Medicare Prescription Drug Plan (Part D) unless you have a creditable plan provided through your employer or a spouse's employer or a creditable COBRA plan. *Failure to enroll* **in a** *Part D plan when you first become eligible could result in a lifetime penalty.* If you chose to enroll in a Medicare Advantage Plan that includes prescription drug coverage, you do not need a separate Part D plan. *See pp. 86-90, "Part D (Medicare Prescription Drug Program)."*

3rd - You should consider enrolling in a Supplemental Medicare Plan (Medigap) unless you have a health insurance plan provided by an employer (or spouse's employer) that will cover you after retirement. If you are uncertain, ask the employer or health insurance carrier. Be aware that Medigap enrollment guidelines are very time sensitive. *Failure to enroll within your protected enrollment period could become very costly. You also risk being denied Medigap coverage* **based on pre-existing conditions.** Unlike health insurance under the Affordable Care Act, insurers in most states can refuse to issue Medicare beneficiaries a Medigap plan based on pre-existing conditions. Some states have more lenient guidelines but be sure to check with your local Agency on Aging before refusing a Medigap plan at the time you first qualify. If you enroll in a Medicare Advantage Plan, do not enroll in a Medigap plan. *See pp. 92-96, "Supplemental Medicare Insurance."*

Medicare Reimbursement

Medicare will reimburse your doctors under the following terms:

Assignment. Physician agrees to accept the Medicare approved amount as the full amount for the service performed. You are responsible for the other 20% unless you have a Medigap or other secondary health insurance plan that will pay it. For example, if the doctor bills Medicare $100 for his service, and Medicare decides it is worth only $80, Medicare will pay 80% of the $80 which is $64. If the doctor accepts assignment, you are responsible for only 20% of the $80 which is $16 (instead of 20% of the $100 billed to Medicare). If you have another insurance plan that pays the 20%, you will have no out-of-pocket costs.

Non-Participating Provider. Physician can charge up to 15% more (called "Excess Charges") than the Medicare approved amount which you must pay plus your 20% copay unless you have an insurance plan that will pay it. Using the same example as above, a non-participating provider would be allowed to bill you an additional 15% on the Medicare approved amount of $80 resulting in Excess Charges of $12. If you have a Medigap plan or other health insurance plan that covers Excess Charges, you would have no out-of-pocket costs. If your Medigap plan or other plan does not cover the excess, then you would be responsible for the $12.

Opt-Out Doctors. These doctors are not subject to Medicare law. Patients are asked to sign a private contract stating they are responsible for paying the entire bill.

You can appeal Medicare reimbursement decisions as follows:

Original Medicare. You will be mailed a Medicare Summary Notice (MSN) every three months. The MSN lists all the services billed to Medicare on your behalf during that three-month period. If you set up a Medicare account at www.mymedicare.gov, you will be able to request your MSN electronically. Be sure to review your MSN. If you see that Medicare was billed for a service you did not receive, contact the medical provider to get it corrected. If you disagree with Medicare's decision to not cover a service, you may file an appeal. Follow the instructions included with your MSN. Your appeal must be in writing and submitted to the Medicare Claims Office. The claims office address will be on your MSN. You have 120 days in which to file your appeal.

Medicare Health Plan. This could be a Medicare Advantage Plan or other health care plan outside Original Medicare. Appeal instructions will be included with the benefit notice mailed to you from your plan. Follow appeal instructions if you disagree with any items listed on your summary.

Medicare Prescription Drug Plan. You may file an appeal if Medicare denies coverage for a prescribed drug or requires you to pay more than you think you should pay. You will usually become aware of this at the time you purchase your prescription. Your pharmacist can give you instructions on how to contact your Medicare drug plan. At that point, you may instruct your drug plan to provide an explanation as to why they denied coverage for the drug or why your cost is so high. Your doctor may also ask the drug plan to grant you an exception.

The *Medicare & You* handbook is a great source of information regarding your benefit coverage and how to file an appeal. Also, check the website www.Medicare.gov/appeals.

Part C (Medicare Advantage Plans)

Medicare Advantage Plans (also known as Medicare Managed Plans) and often referred to as MA plans are offered by private insurance companies under contract with Medicare. You have the option of leaving original Medicare to enroll in a single plan that can handle all your health insurance needs, including a prescription drug plan if offered. You must continue to pay the Part B Medicare premium in addition to the premium for the Medicare Advantage Plan. If the Part C plan does not offer prescription drug coverage, you will need to enroll in a separate plan and pay the Part D premium as well as the Part B and Part C premiums. Currently, these plans seem to work well in cities that have large networks of health care providers but may not work well in rural communities. Before you choose to enroll in a Medicare Advantage Plan, check with your local health care providers and the hospital(s) to ask if they accept the plans being sold in your area.

Types of Medicare Advantage Plans
- *Health Maintenance Organization (HMO).*
  - Generally, you must use doctors who are in an approved network. If you use out-of-network doctors, you pay the entire cost
  - Might offer drug coverage
  - Usually need a primary care doctor
  - Usually need a referral to a specialist
- *Preferred Provider Organization (PPO).*
  - Prefer in-network doctors, but you may use out-of-network doctors at a higher cost
  - Might offer drug coverage
  - Do not need a primary care doctor
  - Usually does not require a referral to a specialist
- *Private Fee-for-Service Plans (PFFS).*
  - Can go to any Medicare-approved doctor that accepts the plan
  - Might offer drug coverage
  - Do not need a primary care doctor
  - Not required to have a referral to a specialist
- *Special Needs Plan (SNP).*
  These plans are for special groups such as people in nursing homes, people with chronic health issues such as diabetes, chronic heart failure, dementia, HIV/AIDS.
  - Plan must provide prescription drug coverage
  - You must have a primary care doctor
  - You usually need a referral to see a specialist
- *HMO Point-of-Service Plans (HMOPOS).*
  - Plans allow out-of-network service at a higher copayment or coinsurance.
- *Medical Savings Account (MSA).*
  - High deductible plans that are like Health Savings Accounts (no drug coverage).

To evaluate Medicare Advantage Plans, go to www.Medicare.gov and click on "Find Health and Drug Plans." Enter your zip code. Complete Step 1. Complete the next screen to see a list of MA plans in your area. For more information, you may contact your local State Health Insurance Program representative (SHIP). To locate your SHIP representative, you may call 1-877-839-2675 or access at https://shiptacenter.org. You may also call Medicare at 1-800-633-4227 (TTY 1-800-486-2048).

Medicare allows you a one-time "trial rights" period to try a Medicare Advantage Plan. The rules are very specific. It must be your first time in a Medicare Advantage Plan. You have 12 months in which to try it. If you want to go back to Original Medicare, you can drop it within that 12-month period without penalty. If you go back to Original Medicare, you should consider enrolling in a Supplemental Medicare Plan (Medigap). *See Chapter 12, pp. 92-96, "Supplemental Medicare Plans."*

When to Enroll
Enrollment Periods for Medicare Advantage Plans (MA Plans)
- During your Medicare Initial Enrollment Period. *See p. 79, for IEP Table.*
- During your Medicare General Enrollment Period (January 1 – March 31) if enrolling in Part B at the same time. Coverage is effective July 1 of that year.
- Between October 15 – December 7. Coverage will be effective January 1st of the following year.

Special Enrollment Periods
Special situations that permit changing a Medicare Advantage Plan
- Move out of your plan's service area.
- Loss of Medicaid (your state's health care plan for those with limited income and resources).
- Become eligible for Social Security's Extra Help program or lose your eligibility for Extra Help. Extra Help is available to those who qualify for prescription drug assistance under Medicare. *See p. 86, "Extra Help, aka Limited Income Subsidy."*
- Become institutionalized.

Changes you can make during your MA Open Enrollment Period (January 1- March 31)
- Switch to a different Medicare Advantage Plan.
- Disenroll from your MA Plan to return to Original Medicare.
Note: Only one change is allowed during this period. The change becomes effective the month following your request.

There are other types of Medicare health plans available in some areas. Obtain information by contacting your local State Health Insurance Assistance Program (SHIP) representative. You may locate your SHIP by calling 1-877-839-2675 or through their website https://shiptacenter.org.

Caution: *Because there are so many factors involved with coverage, costs, and enrollment periods, it is best to seek counsel before enrolling in plans outside of Original Medicare. Many communities sponsor workshops on Original Medicare and other types of Medicare health insurance plans. You may check with your local Agency on Aging (usually a county affiliation) to ask for assistance or call your SHIP. See contact information above.*

Part D (Medicare Prescription Drug Program)

Medicare has contracts with private insurance companies to offer prescription drug coverage for beneficiaries who choose to enroll. **It is optional but highly recommended**. The drug costs are subsidized by the federal government. The prescription drug plans (PDPs) vary in drug formularies (drugs that are covered by the plan), premium costs, deductibles, and copays. Anyone who is eligible for Medicare Part A and/or Part B is eligible for prescription drug coverage.

<u>Premium Costs</u> - The insurance company determines the monthly premium cost for each plan. You will pay that premium unless one of the following applies:

- **Late Enrollment**.
  If you fail to enroll in a timely manner, you could be assessed a penalty increase of 1% for each month beyond the month you should have enrolled. That penalty is applied to your premium (no matter what plan you are in) for the rest of your life.

- **Extra Help, aka as Limited Income Subsidy (LIS).** A federal program administered by the Social Security Administration that can help reduce your drug plan costs. You must meet certain income and resource requirements. You may do an application for Extra Help online at **<u>www.socialsecurity.gov/extrahelp</u>** or call Social Security's 800# service to schedule an appointment, or contact your State Health Insurance Assistance Program (SHIP) representative. Locate your SHIP representative by calling 1-877-839-2675 or access at **<u>https://shiptacenter.org</u>**. You may also call Medicare's 800# service.

- **Medicaid (known by a different name in some states).** This is a state program, federally subsidized, to help people of low income and resources with their health care needs. If you qualify for Medicare Part D and are covered by the Medicaid program, your prescription drug plan costs will be greatly reduced. To check your eligibility for Medicaid, contact your local Department of Social Services. Check online for "your state and county Department of Social Services" or at **<u>www.Medicare.gov/contacts</u>**."

    Note: While the two programs listed above are available nationwide, there are sometimes *local* programs that assist with the costs of the prescription drug plans. Contact your State Health Insurance Assistance Program (SHIP) representative about programs in your area by calling 1-877-839-2675 or access **<u>https://shiptacenter.org</u>** or you may call Medicare's 800# service.

- **Higher Income Bracket.** See the chart on the next page to determine if your Part D premiums will be higher based on your income. If you experience a life-changing event that could reduce your premium surcharge, you may submit a request to Social Security, or the Railroad Board if you are a railroad beneficiary. Some life-changing events are marriage, loss of income, divorce, and death of spouse. Access *Form SSA-44* (Medicare Income-Related Monthly Adjustment Amount) at **<u>https://www.ssdfacts.com/forms/SSA-44.pdf</u>**. Download the form, complete it, and submit it with proof of the change to your local Social Security office or mail it to the Railroad Board. For more information, contact Social Security at 1-800-772-1213 (TTY 1-877-486-2048), RRB at 1-877-772-5772 (TTY 1-312-751-4701).

Income-Related Monthly Adjustment Amount (IRMAA) for Part D Plans

2019 Part D Premiums based on your 2017 filing status and taxable income			
Single – filed individual tax return	**Married – filed joint tax return**	**Married - filed separate tax return**	**You pay each month (in 2019)**
$85,000 or less	$170,000 or less	$85,000 or less	Your plan premium
$85,001 - $107,000	$170,001 - $214,000	N/A	$12.40 + your plan premium
$107,001 - $133,500	$214,001 - $267,000	N/A	$31.90 + your plan premium
$133,501 - $160,000	$267,001 - $320,000	N/A	$51.40 + your plan premium
$160,001 - <$500,000	$320,001 - <$750,000	above $85,000 and less than $415,000	$70.90 + your plan premium
$500,000 and above	$750,000 and above	$415,000 and above	$77.40 + your plan premium

Other Out-of-Pocket Costs. Drugs are priced by tiers, with Tier 1 being the least expensive (generic drugs); Tier 2 is Preferred Brand; Tier 3 is Non-Preferred Brand; and Tier 4 is for Specialty drugs (the most expensive). If your doctor can prescribe generic drugs, you will have lower out-of-pocket costs. If your doctor decides a generic drug won't work for you and he/she must prescribe a brand name drug, be sure to look at the different plans carefully to select one that covers all your drugs. Your doctor can also request the drug plan to lower your copay. Should you learn that a prescription you are on is not covered or is cost prohibitive, contact a State Health Insurance Assistance Program (SHIP) representative to ask if there are programs to help pay for that drug. Locate your local SHIP representative by calling 1-877-839-2675 or access at https://shiptacenter.org or call Medicare's 800# service.

- **Copay.** A copayment is a set amount (e.g. $10) for all drugs in a tier.
- **Coinsurance.** A set percentage you pay for your drugs (e.g. 25%).

Part D Benefit Parameters. The Centers for Medicare and Medicaid Services (CMS) establishes thresholds for a beneficiary's out-of-pocket costs. These amounts can increase annually.

- **Deductible.** The maximum deductible allowed for 2019 is $415. Almost every drug plan has a deductible and the amount can vary from plan to plan. If you choose one with a deductible, you will have to pay 100% out of pocket towards your drugs until that deductible is met. Exceptions might exist for beneficiaries who are getting help through a financial assistance program. There are variations of financial help. You should apply for any assistance program for which you might qualify prior to or at the time you enroll in a drug plan. To learn more about programs in your area, contact the State Health Insurance Program (SHIP) at 1-877-839-2675 or access at **https://shiptacenter.org** to locate your local representative. You may also call Medicare's 800# service to get the phone number.

- **Initial Coverage Period (ICP).** The maximum out-of-pocket costs during the ICP for 2019 is $3820. Once you have met your deductible, you enter the Initial Coverage Period (ICP). During the ICP you have a 25% coinsurance toward the prescription drug cost. After you reach the $3820 in out-of-pocket costs for your drugs, you move to the Coverage Gap.

- **Coverage Gap (aka Donut Hole).** In 2019, the maximum out-of-pocket costs during the Coverage Gap is $5100; however, the out-of-pocket costs for brand name drugs is greatly reduced in 2019. You will pay only 25% for brand name drugs but you will receive credit toward your out-of-pocket cost at 95% of the retail cost. You will pay 37% of the retail costs for generic drugs. You receive the same 37% of the generic drug cost towards your out-of-pocket total. Following is an example of how your out-of-pocket cost is calculated.

  Example: Donna purchased two prescription drugs from her pharmacy through her Part D plan. One drug was a brand name drug that retailed for $100. Her cost is 25% of the retail cost; she paid $25. She also purchased a generic drug that had a retail value of $20. Her costs is 37% of the retail costs; she paid $7.40. In addition to her drug costs, the pharmacy charged her a dispensing fee of $3.00. Of the dispensing fee, 25% can be credited toward out-of-pocket costs.
  Her out-of-pocket costs is calculated as follows:

  $95.00 – Brand name drug
  7.40 – Generic drug
  .75 – 25% of the dispensing fee
  $103.15 – Total credited to Donna's out-of-pocket costs

- **Catastrophic Coverage.** Once you meet the maximum costs for the Coverage Gap ($5100), your costs drop to only 5% of the retail drug costs.
  Note: At the end of each year, you may determine future year deductibles, coinsurance, copays, and coverage gap parameters, by going to Medicare's website **www.medicare.gov** and type "Part D plan costs" in the Search Box. You can also get up-to-date information from your local State Health Insurance Program (SHIP) office. Locate your local SHIP representative by calling 1-877-839-2675 or access at **https://shiptacenter.org**. You may also call Medicare's 800# service to get the phone number.

Part D Enrollment Periods

- **Initial Enrollment Period (IEP).** Begins three months before your 65th birthday, includes the month you turn 65, and ends three months after your 65th birthday.

- **General Enrollment Period (GEP).** January 1st - March 31st of each year. If enrolling for Part B of Medicare during the GEP, you may enroll in a Part D plan between April 1st - June 30th of that same year. Your coverage will start July 1st of that year.

- **Open Enrollment Period (OEP).** You can join, switch, or drop your Part D plan between October 15th - December 7th each year. The change is effective January 1st of the next year.

- **Special Enrollment Period (SEP).** The SEP is granted for the reasons below. The SEP is usually a 63-day period. Take prompt action to get enrolled in a Part D plan or make a change if losing your current plan.
    - Move out of your plan's service area
    - Lose creditable coverage you had through another plan
    - Qualify for (or lose) Extra Help through Social Security
    - Qualify for Medicaid or lose Medicaid
    - Live in an institution such as a nursing home

- **Five-Star Plans.** If any plans become rated as five-star plans, you may be offered an opportunity to enroll in one outside the regular enrollment periods.

Exceptions for Enrolling in a Part D Plan:
- You are covered under a Medicare Advantage plan
- You have creditable coverage through an employer plan or spouse's employer plan
- You have prescription drug coverage as a military veteran (through the VA)
- You have coverage through TRICARE (must also have Medicare Part B)

***Caution*:** If you do not enroll in a drug plan when you are first eligible, you can be assessed a 1% penalty for each month following the date you should have enrolled and the date your enrollment is effective. The penalty lasts for a lifetime. Even if you are not taking medications, consider enrolling in the least expensive plan available to avoid future penalties.

Part D Enrollment

- The State Health Insurance Assistance Program (SHIP) offers free counseling services for Medicare and Medicare-related issues. You can get help enrolling in a prescription drug plan. More importantly, you can be screened for programs that might assist you in paying the cost of your prescription plan. To locate your SHIP representative, call 1-877-839-2675 or go to https://shiptacenter.org.
- Call Medicare at 1-800-633-4227 (TTY 1-800-486-2048). Generally, someone can help you over the phone. Social Security <u>cannot</u> enroll you in a Part D plan. Social Security can, however, enroll you in the Extra Help program which helps pay Part D costs.
- Online at www.medicare.gov.
    - On the Home screen, click on tab "Find health & drug plans."
    - On next screen, enter your zip code in the "Basic Search" box. Hit *Enter*.
    - Complete Step 1 of 4 screen as it applies to you, then select "Continue to Plan Results."
    - Complete Step 2 of 4 screen by listing your prescriptions. Complete pop-up screen for each drug. After you enter your first drug, you will see the Step 2 of 4 screen re-appear with a **Drug List ID and password** in the "My Current Profile" box. *Please record*

this information or print the sheet and keep in a safe place. Any time you re-enter the Plan Finder, you can simply use your ID and password to pull up your drug list. You will find this especially helpful when checking the new drug plans each year during the Open Enrollment Period (October 15-December 7). **You should do a new search every year to be sure your plan is still the best plan for you. The drug plans can change from year to year** and sometimes during the year.

o   On Step 2 of 4 screen continue listing prescriptions until your drug list is complete.
o   Complete Step 3 of 4 screen by listing two pharmacies you prefer, then select "Continue to Plan Results." *Be aware drug prices can vary from pharmacy to pharmacy.*
o   Complete Step 4 of 4 screen "Refine Your Plan Results." Then select "Continue to Plan Results."
o   On the next screen, scroll down to "Compare Plans." It will list ten plans per page. Note the "?" in the title of each column. You may click on "?" to get a detailed explanation of the information you see in that column.
o   Click in the block in front of plans that you want more information on. You may compare up to three plans at a time.
o   After you select the plans you want to view, select "Compare Plans" option.
o   On the next screen, "Your Plan Comparison," you will see the information for each plan you selected. You may click on "?" to get more details.
o   Finally click on "Enroll" for the plan you want. You may also call the 800# service for the plan. They have agents who can assist you with enrollment.
o   Finally, follow the remaining prompts. ***Print your enrollment letter***.

Note: *Do not select the option to have the Part D premium taken from your Social Security benefit*. This can create problems for you if you change your plan the following year.

Within ten days of completing your online application, you should receive a letter confirming your enrollment. Within another two to four weeks you will receive the enrollment package from the insurance company. In it, *you will find your prescription drug card, a booklet that shows the drug formulary (list of drugs covered by the plan) and instructions on how you can pay your monthly premium*. Consider taking your drug formulary with you when you visit medical providers. Should they need to write a prescription for you, they can prescribe one that is on your formulary.

When you enroll in a plan, you generally must remain in that plan throughout the year. There are a few exceptions. See previous page for the Part D Special Enrollment Period criteria.

If you are covered by a program that is helping to pay your Part D costs (Extra Help, Medicaid, or other state programs), you are often able to change plans outside the Open Enrollment Period (OEP). Contact your local State Health Insurance Program (SHIP) representative for details. You may locate your SHIP representative by calling 1-877-839-2675 or access at **https://shiptacenterorg**, or you may get the phone number by calling Medicare's 800# service.

Medicare Fraud

Medicare and Medicaid fraud have become a multi-billion-dollar problem. It is estimated that Medicare and Medicaid lost about $60 billion to fraud in 2017. To help combat the problem, the Social Security numbers have been removed from the Medicare cards.

By April 2019, all Medicare beneficiaries will have been mailed a new Medicare card with an eleven-digit identifier made up of numbers and uppercase letters. This will be known as the Medicare Beneficiary Identifier (MBI). Eliminating the Social Security number from the Medicare card will not only help prevent Medicare fraud but will also help protect beneficiaries from identity theft.

It is recommended that you carry your Medicare card with you only when you are visiting a health care provider and return it to a secure place in your home after your visit.

Be Proactive
Medicare Health Insurance (Part A & B)
- Keep a personal record of all your medical visits. Include the reason for your visit, the date, time, name, address, and phone number of the health care provider (doctor, chiropractor, physical therapist, etc.). You may also verify details of your health care visits online by setting up your own Medicare account at www.mymedicare.gov.
- Compare your personal record with the Medicare Summary Notice (MSN) that is mailed every three months. The MSN lists all the providers to whom Medicare made a payment and the amount of the payment. If it does not agree with your records, call the provider in question. If there is an error, ask the provider to correct it. If they do not correct it, contact Medicare 1-800-633-4227 (TTY 877-486-2048). If you suspect Medicare fraud, contact the Office of Inspector General (OIG) 1-800-447-8477 (TTY 1-800-337-4950). Other types of medical fraud should be reported to the Federal Trade Commission at 1-877-438-4338 (TTY 1-866-653-4261) or at www.identitytheft.gov.
- Question your health care provider if you think unnecessary tests are being requested.
- Guard your Medicare card. Do not give your Medicare Beneficiary Identifier number to anyone other than your medical provider. If you receive a call from Centers for Medicare and Medicaid Services to do a survey (they occasionally do telephone surveys), they will not ask for your MBI, your Social Security number, nor your date of birth. They have access to that information on their computers. Your participation in the survey is optional. If you do not feel comfortable doing it, you may decline.

Medicare Prescription Drug Coverage (Part D)
- Keep a record of all prescriptions written for you by your doctors.
- Keep a record of the date you filled your prescriptions and the pharmacy or mail order company you used.
- Compare your records to the Explanation of Benefits (EOB) that is mailed to you after each month in which you fill a prescription. If there is a discrepancy, check with the provider first. If the discrepancy is not resolved, contact Medicare at 1-800-633-4227 (TTY 1-877-486-2048).

Chapter 12

Supplemental Medicare Insurance (Medigap)

Medigap plans are offered by private insurance companies under contract with Medicare and your State Health Insurance agency to provide supplemental health insurance to Medicare beneficiaries. The plans are most commonly referred to as Medigap plans because they are designed to help cover the gaps in Medicare, i.e., the deductible, copay, and coinsurance that Medicare does not cover.

You must have Part A and B of Medicare. You must enroll with the insurance company, not through Social Security or Medicare, and your premium is paid directly to the insurance company. When you enroll in a standardized Medigap plan and pay your premiums timely, you may stay in that plan for the rest of your life if you wish.

Consider enrolling in a Medigap plan within the first six months of your Part B entitlement (known as your Open Enrollment Period) unless you qualify for a Special Enrollment Period (see next page). During the Open Enrollment Period for Part B you have Guaranteed Issue Rights which allow you to enroll in any Medigap plan you choose without going through medical underwriting. Medical underwriting allows the insurance company to refuse you coverage based on certain medical standards. In other words, pre-existing conditions might disqualify you unless you are in your Part B Open Enrollment Period or a Special Enrollment Period. Some states (California, Connecticut, Missouri, Oregon and New York) have fewer restrictions but make sure you know what is required in your state. And some insurers are more lenient than others.

What is not covered by Medigap
If Medicare does not cover it, Medigap will not cover it. The following are not covered:
- Vision and dental care (exception for one pair of eyeglasses for cataract surgery with intraocular implant)
- Hearing aids
- Private-duty nursing
- Outpatient prescription drugs (will be covered under Part D of Medicare)
- Long Term Care

To learn about your state's Medigap plans, you may contact several sources
- Each state has a State Health Insurance Assistance Program (SHIP). Locate your SHIP representative by calling 1-877-839-2675 or access at **https://shiptacenter.org**. You may also call Medicare's 800# service to get your local SHIP number. Also ask your SHIP representative if there are any Medicare workshops or seminars in your area.
- You may check online at **www.Medicare.gov**. Type "Medigap Plans" in the Search Box, select "Find a Plan," enter your Zip Code and follow instructions on screens. You may also call Medicare at 1-800-633-4227 (TTY 1-877-486-2048) for assistance.
- And, last, you may contact insurance agencies in your area to ask if they sell Medigap plans If so, ask for quotes on the different types of plans. *See pp. 94- 96, "Medicare Supplemental Insurance Plans (Medigap)."*

Medigap Enrollment

As a result of health insurance changes that came out of the Affordable Care Act in 2010, many Medicare beneficiaries are under the mistaken impression that insurance companies cannot refuse them due to pre-existing conditions. Therefore, understanding the Medigap enrollment periods is very important. ***Caution:*** *If you do not enroll in a Medigap plan during your Open Enrollment Period (OEP), the* <u>*insurance companies in most states can refuse you coverage based on pre-existing conditions.*</u> *This could become very costly should you ever experience serious health problems. There is only one Open Enrollment Period for Medigap (begins when your Part B of Medicare starts and ends six months later). Exception: Disability beneficiaries who have Medicare before age 65. They will have a new Open Enrollment Period at age 65.*

To Enroll in a Medigap Plan
- You must have Part A & B of Medicare
  Note: If you receive Medicare coverage based on a Social Security disability, check with your State Health Insurance Assistance Program (SHIP) representative to determine if you can enroll in a Medigap plan in your state. Not all states offer Medigap plans to people under age 65. Locate your local SHIP representative by calling 1-877-839-2675 or access at <u>https://shiptacenter.org</u>. You may also call Medicare's 800# service.

When to Enroll in a Medigap Plan
- **Open Enrollment Period (OEP).** The OEP begins the first month of Part B coverage and ends six months later. During the OEP, you may purchase any Medicare Supplemental Plan (Medigap Plan) you want without medical underwriting. This is known as your Guaranteed Issue Rights period. Beyond this period, the insurance companies have the right to refuse you unless you qualify for a Special Enrollment Period (SEP).
  Note: If you have been without health insurance preceding your OEP for Medigap, the insurance company may delay Medigap coverage up to six months for a pre-existing condition.
- **Special Enrollment Period (SEP).** The SEP is a 63-day period that gives you Guaranteed Issue Rights and will allow you to enroll or switch for the following reasons:
  - Medicare beneficiary who kept Part B while under an active employer group health insurance plan (EGHP) and is now losing the employer plan due to retirement or spouse's retirement.
  - Current Medigap plan is being discontinued. You would be notified by the insurer. *Note:* If you move to a different state, call the phone number on the back of your Medigap card to report your new address and bank information. Also, ask if your Medigap premium will change. If you are in a Medigap Select plan (somewhat like an HMO), ask if you need to make a change in your plan after you move.

Always set up direct debit for your Medigap premium. Set up a direct debit from your bank account or authorize a charge to a credit card. If you were to miss a payment, the insurance company could suspend or terminate your coverage. The Medigap insurer(s) can then require you to go through medical underwriting before they will insure you. This could result in higher Medigap premiums or losing Medigap coverage for the rest of your life.

Situations in which you might not need a Medigap Plan
- **Employer Plan.**
  If you retire from a job that allows you to keep your health insurance after retirement (includes federal and some military health insurance plans), the employer plan will act as your "secondary" insurance, which means it could help with your Medicare deductible, copay, and coinsurance. It might also cover some services that Medicare does not cover, i.e., vision and dental. Learn what it covers and what your costs will be. You might find better coverage and costs with a Medigap plan.
- **Medicaid Eligibility.**
  If you are covered under Medicaid, you do not have to buy a Medigap plan. However, if you should lose your Medicaid coverage for any reason, you will likely have to go through medical underwriting before you will be allowed to enroll in a Medigap plan. If you have a Medigap policy and then become eligible for Medicaid, you have a 90-day period in which you may suspend your Medigap policy for up to 2 years. Doing this means you keep the Guaranteed Issue Rights protection but won't have to pay the Medigap premium. Because some doctors don't accept Medicaid, you might prefer to keep the Medigap active so you can go to the doctors you prefer. If you keep the Medigap active, you will have to pay the Medigap premiums. If you choose to suspend the Medigap, call your Medigap insurance provider. The phone number should be on the back of your Medigap insurance card.

Selecting a Supplemental Medicare Plan (Medigap)
Important terms to know in evaluating Medigap coverage.
- *No-age-rated (community-rated)* – Everyone pays the same premium regardless of age if 65 or older. Premium does not automatically go up as you get older.
- *Issue-age-rated* – Premium based on age when purchased. Does not go up automatically as you get older.
- *Attained-age-rated* – Premium is based on current age. Premium goes up automatically as you get older.
- *Assignment* – Physician agrees to accept the Medicare approved amount as the full amount for the service performed. You are responsible for the other 20% unless you have a Medigap plan or other insurance that will pay it.
- *Non-Participating Provider* – Physician can charge up to 15% more (called "Excess Charges") than the Medicare approved amount which you must pay plus your 20% co-pay. Some Medigap plans will pay the Excess Charges.
- *Opt-Out Doctors* – These doctors are not subject to Medicare law. Patients are asked to sign a private contract stating they are responsible for paying the entire bill. Medicare and Medigap will not reimburse for any portion of the bill. The rule is that if Medicare doesn't cover the service, neither will Medigap.

How to Evaluate the Table on page 96:
- *Across the top of the Table*, you see alpha designations. The letters represent the types of Medigap plans. Please note that the A, B, C, and D plans are not the same as the Medicare A, B, C, and D plans. This creates a lot of confusion for people. The Medigap A, B, C, and D plans help with the deductibles, copays, and coinsurances that Medicare Part A and B do not cover.

- *Down the left column* of the Table, you see the types of service covered by Medicare.
- *In the rows/blocks in the body of the Table*, you see percentages listed under the columns (designated by a letter of the alphabet). The percentage indicates how much of the cost Medigap will pay for that service.
  Note: *As of 2020, the C and F plans will no longer be sold. This change will not affect people already enrolled in the C and F plans.*

Your Out-of-Pocket costs (in addition to your monthly premiums)
- ***Example of a medical bill from a doctor who accepts Assignment:***
  If you have a Medigap G plan and your doctor bills Medicare for $100 for a Part B service, Medicare will pay 80% of the $100. That means your Medigap plan will pay the $20 coinsurance in full (100%). You would have no out-of-pocket cost. If Medicare decided the service listed above was worth only $80 (not the $100 that was billed), Medicare would pay only 80% of the $80, which is $64. The Medigap plan will pay $16 and your doctor will accept that as payment in full.
- ***Example of a medical bill from a doctor who does <u>not</u> accept Assignment***:
  If the doctor does not accept assignment (Non-Participating) you could be responsible for a 15% Excess Charge. The Excess Charge can never be more than 15% of the Medicare approved amount. In the above example, it would be 15% of the $80 or $12 more, which would be your out-of-pocket costs. However, if you have a Medigap G plan that covers 100% of excess charges you would have no additional costs.
- ***Example of a medical bill from an Opt-out-Doctor:***
  If the doctor is an Opt-out-Doctor (meaning he does not accept Medicare) you would be responsible for 100% of the charges. Medicare will not pay anything nor will any Medigap policy.

Medicare Supplemental Insurance Plans (Medigap)

Benefits	A	B	C	D	F*	G	K**	L***	M	N****
Medicare part A coinsurance and hospital costs (up to an additional 365 days after Medicare benefits are used)	100%	100%	100%	100%	100%	100%	100%	100%	100%	100%
Medicare Part B coinsurance or copayment	100%	100%	100%	100%	100%	100%	50%	75%	100%	100%
Blood (first 3 pints)	100%	100%	100%	100%	100%	100%	50%	75%	100%	100%
Part A hospice care coinsurance or copayment	100%	100%	100%	100%	100%	100%	50%	75%	100%	100%
Skilled nursing facility care coinsurance			100%	100%	100%	100%	50%	75%	100%	100%
Part A deductible		100%	100%	100%	100%	100%	50%	75%	50%	100%
Part B deductible			100%		100%					
Part B Excess					100%	100%				
Foreign travel emergency			80%	80%	80%	80%			80%	80%

*Plan F: Also offers a high-deductible plan. If you choose a high F plan, you must pay the deductible before Medicare pays towards your health-care costs. In 2019, the high deductible amount is $2,300.

**Plan K: Out-of-pocket limit is $5,560. ***Plan L: Out-of-pocket limit is $2,780

****Plan N: Pays 100% of your part B coinsurance but you must pay up to a $20 copay for office visits and can also be charged a $50 copay for emergency room visits unless you are admitted.

Note: Standardized Medigap plans for Massachusetts, Minnesota, and Wisconsin differ from the above. Information for these specific states can be obtained from medicare.gov/find-a-plan. Enter your zip code, go to "Additional Tools" (in right pane), select "Find and Compare Medigap Policies."

Representative Payee Procedures

Social Security and Supplemental Security Income beneficiaries (of legal age) are presumed capable of managing their own benefits. However, there are times when a beneficiary might need assistance in handling his/her funds. The issue of capability often arises when a relative, a close friend, or a social service agency reports a concern about the beneficiary's ability to manage his/her own benefits.

In this situation, the Social Security Administration has an obligation to investigate the person's ability to make good choices for himself/herself regarding the use of Social Security benefits. If the beneficiary is found incapable, the Social Security Administration must appoint someone to manage the benefits. This person is called a Representative Payee.

The policy for determining capability is as follows:

1. If there is a legal decision stating the person is incapable, Social Security must appoint someone to handle the beneficiary's benefits.

2. If there is no legal decision but it appears a determination needs to be made regarding capability, a Social Security Claims Specialist can ask for the primary doctor's name and address and send a request for a medical opinion on the beneficiary's capability.

3. If there is no legal decision and no doctor to contact, the next step would be for a Claims Specialist (in the local Social Security Administration office) to meet with the beneficiary. The beneficiary will be asked several questions. If during that interview, it is determined that the beneficiary appears disoriented or confused, has difficulty communicating, and lacks the ability to make good judgments, the Claims Specialist can make a *lay* determination to appoint a Representative Payee.

If the Social Security Administration determines the beneficiary is incapable, the agency will locate a person who is willing to manage the benefits. There are very strict standards that must be met before someone can be appointed to handle another person's benefits. It must be a person who is deemed trustworthy. The Representative Payee appointed is often a close relative, a close friend or an agency.

The Social Security benefit can be used only for the beneficiary's needs. The Representative Payee has a responsibility to report any changes that would apply to the type of benefits the person is receiving. See "Changes to be Reported" at the end of each chapter on benefits.

The Social Security Administration requires the representative payee to provide an annual report of how the beneficiary's funds were used.

Chapter 14

Overpayments

One of the most upsetting experiences Social Security beneficiaries can have is to receive a letter notifying them they were paid too much in benefits and they must reimburse Social Security for the overpaid funds. The overpayment letter explains how the overpayment occurred, the months benefits were overpaid, the amount of overpayment, and the action that will be taken if the beneficiary does not contact the agency within 30 days. The letter includes information on how to file for a waiver of the overpayment and/or request a Reconsideration, and also states the time period in which to file the waiver and/or appeal.

While there are many reasons that an overpayment can occur, the most frequent reason is due to non-reporting of work and earnings – especially for those who are receiving Disability Benefits. To avoid overpayments, be sure to read the *Changes to be Reported* at the end of each benefits chapter. Prompt reporting of these changes can help you avoid an overpayment.

How to Resolve an Overpayment
Call the Social Security Administration at 1-800-772-1213 (TTY 1-800-325-0778) to discuss your letter.
- If you agree with the overpayment, discuss how you would like to repay it. Most people cannot afford to repay in one lump sum or to have their entire benefit withheld. You may ask to have a smaller amount withheld from your monthly benefit or, if you are not currently receiving benefits, you may set up a payment plan.
- If you disagree with the overpayment decision, you may contact Social Security to file for a Reconsideration. You will be mailed *Form SSA-561*.
- You may ask to file a waiver. You will be mailed *Form SSA-632BK* to complete. You will be required to provide information (and proof) of income and resources. Requesting a waiver does not mean it will be granted.
  - Two requirements must be met before a waiver can be approved:
    - You must be without fault in causing the overpayment, <u>and</u>
    - Recovery or adjustment of the overpayment would defeat the purpose of Social Security or be against equity and good conscience. A Claims Specialist can explain these requirements in detail.
  Note: Not understanding how or why you were overpaid does not meet the definition of "without fault."

If the waiver is denied, you may request a Personal Conference. At a Personal Conference (face-to-face or by phone) you may speak directly with a Claims Specialist to review how the overpayment occurred and to provide any proofs that support your waiver request. If, after the Personal Conference, your waiver request is again denied, you have the right to file a Hearing (*Form SSA-501*). You may appear before an Administrative Law Judge to give testimony as to why you feel you should not have to repay the overpayment. If your Hearing is denied, you will be advised of your right to file for an Appeals Council review (Form HA-520). *See Chapter 10, pp. 71-73, "Appeals Process."*

Paying Taxes on your Social Security Benefits

The Internal Revenue Service (IRS) is responsible for assessing and collecting taxes from Social Security benefits. Social Security employees are trained to direct individuals to contact IRS to get questions answered regarding tax liability. Each January, Social Security mails to you a Benefit Statement *(Form SSA-1099)* showing the amount of your prior year benefits. When you get your prior year IRS tax preparation forms, (your Form 1040 with instructions), you will see a page titled "Social Security Benefits Worksheet - Lines 5a and 5b." Use this worksheet to help you determine how much of your benefits are taxable. You may also request the Form SSA-1099 through your personal Social Security account at **www.socialsecurity.gov/myaccount**.

FORMULA: 1st – Calculate your Adjusted Gross Income (Form 1040, page 2, Line 7)
           2nd – Add Nontaxable interest
           3rd – Add ½ of your Social Security benefits
           4th – This total equals your <u>COMBINED INCOME</u>

If filing a federal return as an individual and COMBINED INCOME is:

Between $25,000 - $34,000   up to 50% of your Social Security benefit could be taxable

More than $34,000   up to 85% of your Social Security benefit could be taxable

If filing a joint return for you and your spouse and COMBINED INCOME is:

Between $32,000 - $44,000   up to 50% of your Social Security benefit could be taxable

More than $44,000   up to 85% of your Social Security benefit could be taxable

If you are married but filing separate tax returns, you will probably pay taxes on your benefits.

You may ask to have federal taxes withheld from your Social Security benefit at the time you file. Your options for withholding taxes are as follows: 7%, 10%, 12%, or 22%.

If you are already receiving benefits or want to make a change in the percentage of reduction, call the IRS to ask for a *Voluntary Withholding Request (Form W-4V)* or download the form from **www.IRS.gov**. All questions regarding your tax liability must be directed to IRS at 1-800-829-1040 (TTY 1-800-829-4059).

Chapter 16

Resources of Interest

Dental, Vision, and Hearing – Medicare does not provide coverage for these services. The National Council on Aging (NCOA), however, has provided information to help you locate agencies and organizations that might assist you. Check out their website to review all the helpful tips, tools, and service(s) they provide. Go to www.NCOA.org.

Dental

- **Community Health Centers** – provide health services and dental care to those with limited income. To locate one near you go to http://findahealthcenter.hrsa.gov.
- **American Dental Association** – can provide you with a list of schools (university or community college) that have a dental school program. They often provide discounted dental services by the students who are in training. Go to www.ada.org/267.aspx or the American Dental Hygienists Association at www.adha.org/dental-hygiene-programs.
- **Dental Lifeline Network** – provides services to vulnerable adults, including the disabled and elderly. Go to http://dentallifeline.org/.

Hearing

- **Foundation for Sight and Sound** has a Help America Hear Program that provides Hearing aids for people (including children) with limited financial resources.
  Go to https://www.foundationforsightandsound.org/.
- **Lions Club** – contact your local Lions Club to ask if they sponsor the Affordable Hearing Aid Project. This program offers affordable hearing aids in partnership with Rexton, Inc. (a company that manufactures hearing aids). To find a local chapter, go to www.lcif.org.
- **Sertoma** – a civic organization that locates help for people with hearing problems. Go to www.sertoma.org/.

Vision

- **Eye Care America** – provides free eye exams for limited-income people who qualify. Go to www.eyecareamerica.org.
- **Lions Club** – provides some services to assist people with visual impairment. To locate a chapter near you, go to www.lcif.org.
- **Vision USA** – provides free eye exams for low-income Americans who have no insurance. Go to www.aoafoundation.org/vision.
- **Mission Cataract USA** – provides free cataract surgery to those without insurance. Go to www.missioncataractusa.org.

Health Insurance Issues:
State Health Insurance Assistance Program (SHIP)
Many questions regarding Medicare, Supplemental Medicare Plans (Medigap), the prescription drug program, and the Extra Help program can be answered by the SHIP representative in your area. To locate your SHIP representative, you may call 1-877-839-2675 or access the website at https://shiptacenter.org. You may also call Medicare at 1-800-633-4227 (TTY 1-877-486-2048) to ask for the SHIP number.

State/County Departments of Social Services
Locate their phone number in your local phone directory or you may check online for your state and county Department of Social Services, or at www.medicare.gov/contacts . These agencies often have programs that can help with Medicare premiums, co-insurance, and copays.

Office of Personnel Management (OPM)
Federal retirees may get information about Federal Employee Health Benefits (FEHB).
1-888-767-6738 (TTY 1-800-877-8339)
https://opm.gov

Active employees must contact the Benefits Officer
https://apps.opm.gov/abo

Railroad Retirement Board (RRB)
If you are receiving benefits from the Railroad Board, you must call them to determine your eligibility, report changes in your address, phone number, replace your Medicare card, and to report a death.
1-877-772-5772 (TTY 1-312-751-4701)
https://rrb.gov

TRICARE for Life
1-866-773-0404 (TTY 1-866-773-0405)
https://TRICARE.mil/tfl
https://TRICARE4u.com

TRICARE Pharmacy Program
1-877-363-1303 (TTY 1-877-540-6261)
https://mil/pharmacy
https://express-scripts.com/TRICARE

Department of Veterans Affairs
If you have served in the military and have questions about VA benefits, call
1-800-827-1000
https://va.gov

<u>Identity Theft Issues:</u>

Federal Trade Commission Identity Theft Hotline
If you suspect someone is using your Social Security number to obtain credit, or if you suspect you are a victim of medical identity theft, call 1-877-438-4338 (TTY-866-653-4261) <u>www.IdentityTheft.gov</u>

Internal Revenue Service
If you experience problems getting your tax refund, it might be because someone is using your Social Security number to collect money owed to you (or it might be an error). Call 1-800-908-4490 (TTY 1-800-829-4059)
<u>www.irs.gov/uac/Identity-Protection</u>

To monitor your credit report, go to <u>www.annualcreditreport.com</u>

Glossary

Administrative Law Judge (ALJ) – Lawyers trained in Social Security law who are appointed to act as judges to weigh evidence filed in Hearing cases with the Social Security Administration.

Appeal – General term referring to the request for a review of a decision on a claim for Social Security, Supplemental Security Income, and/or Medicare benefits.

Appeals Council Review – Third level of appeal that can be filed on a Hearing decision.

Applicant – Person signing an application for Social Security benefits.

Assignment – Physician agrees to accept the Medicare approved amount as the full amount for the service provided. You are responsible for a 20% copay (unless you have other health insurance).

Auxiliary Benefits – Benefits payable to family members, i.e., spouse and children.

Average Indexed Monthly Earnings (AIME) – The average monthly earnings of the years used in the computation of the benefit (adjusted for inflation).

Benefit Period – A period of time that is defined by Medicare for coverage under Part A. See page 76 for details.

Calendar Quarter – Each year is divided into calendar quarters (January-March, April-June, July-September, October-December) for the purpose of assigning Social Security credits.

Childhood Disability Benefits – Benefits payable on a parent's record to an unmarried child who is/was disabled before age 22.

Claimant –Person for whom a Social Security application is being filed.

Claims Specialist (CS), formerly known as a Claims Representative, – The Social Security representative who is responsible for reviewing applications for Social Security benefits, obtaining all necessary documentation to support the claim, and adjudicating the claim for payment.

Coinsurance – Portion of a medical bill (usually a percentage) that the patient must pay.

Consumer Price Index (CPI-W) – A measurement that is used by the Department of Labor to track annual changes in living costs. It is used to compute the cost of living adjustment (COLA).

Copayment – An assigned dollar amount that must be paid by the patient for a medical service.

Cost of Living Adjustment (COLA) – An annual increase to Social Security and Supplemental Security Income benefits (if approved by Congress).

Creditable Health Insurance – Insurance that Medicare deems to be as good as or better than the coverage that Medicare provides.

Credits (quarters of coverage) – Each credit is based on a dollar value of earnings. Four credits can be earned annually. Forty credits are needed for Retirement Benefits. The number required for disability and survivor benefits can vary depending on age.

Customer Service Representative (CSR), formerly known as a Service Representative – An employee trained in answering questions regarding the Social Security and Supplemental Security Income programs and assisting beneficiaries with their needs after they start receiving benefits.

Deductible – An assigned amount that a person must pay towards their health care costs before the insurance will pay anything.

Delayed Retirement Credits (DRCs) – A percentage of increase added to a full Retirement Benefit amount for each month no benefits are paid between full retirement age and age 70.

Drug Formulary – A list of prescription drugs that are covered by a specific drug plan.

Earnings Test – Amount of earnings allowed for a beneficiary who wants to work while receiving benefits and is not yet full retirement age. Pensions and investment income do not count as earnings.

Earnings/Wages – Remuneration for work/services performed for an employer or from work performed as a self-employed person.

Eligible – Meet the requirements for Social Security benefits, i.e., age and credits needed.

Employer or Union Retiree Plans – Health insurance coverage provided by an employer or union for employees after their retirement.

Entitlement – Meet the requirements for Social Security benefits and have filed an application to receive those benefits.

Extra Help – A program administered by the Social Security Administration that assists in paying costs for a Medicare Prescription Drug plan.

Family Benefits (Dependent Benefits) – Family members (auxiliaries) who are eligible for benefits on the Social Security record of a wage earner.

Family Maximum – Maximum amount of Social Security benefits that can be paid to family members based on a wage earner's entitlement.

Federal Income Contribution Act (FICA) – Federal law that determines the tax amounts employees and employers must pay to earn Social Security and Medicare credits.

Full Retirement Age (FRA) – Age at which a person can receive Social Security benefits without a reduction.

General Enrollment Period (GEP) – The first three months of each calendar year that allows for Medicare enrollment based on certain guidelines.

Government Pension Offset (GPO) – A reduction applied to the Social Security benefit a person receives on another wage earner's record (as a spouse, widow(er), or surviving divorced spouse). This reduction affects those eligible for a pension for which they did not pay Social Security taxes to earn. See example on page 13.

Guaranteed Issue Rights – Rights a Medicare beneficiary has (for a limited period of time) that allows him/her to enroll in a Medigap policy without going through medical underwriting.

Health Savings Account (HSA) – A high-deductible health plan provided through an employer that allows the insured to forgo paying federal income taxes on contributions to the plan account.

Hearing – Second level of appeal requesting a review of a decision on a claim for Social Security, Supplemental Security Income, and/or Medicare benefits.

Impairment Related Work Expenses (IRWE) – Expenses a disabled beneficiary incurs that are necessary for him/her to maintain a job. The expenses can be deducted from the earnings that count against the beneficiary. This is a determination that will be made by a Claims Specialist at the time a Continuing Disability Review is done on a beneficiary's disability record.

Insured Status – The state of having worked and earned sufficient credits to be eligible for benefits.

Lawfully-Admitted Alien – Noncitizens who are authorized by the U.S. Citizenship and Immigration Services to reside in the U.S.

Medicaid – A health insurance program administered by State and County governments (supplemented by federal funds) to provide health care assistance for people with low income and limited resources. It can help reduce Medicare premium and copay costs.

Medical Underwriting – A process insurance companies can use to determine if an individual will be approved or denied health insurance coverage. It can be required for those not meeting Guaranteed Issue Rights for Medigap coverage.

Medicare – Federal health insurance program available to Social Security beneficiaries.

Medicare Advantage Plans (aka Part C) – Insurance plans (sometimes referred to as MA) plans offered by private insurance companies under contract with Medicare that allow you the option to leave "Original Medicare" to enroll in a single plan that handles all your health insurance needs – hospital, medical, and sometimes prescription drug coverage.

Medigap (aka Supplemental Medicare Insurance) – A privately sold insurance that can be purchased to help with deductibles, coinsurance, and copays that Medicare does not cover.

Month of Entitlement (MOE) – The month that an applicant becomes entitled to Social Security or Supplemental Security Income benefits.

Monthly Benefit Amount (MBA) – Social Security amount a beneficiary is due each month. Can be the same amount as the Primary Insurance Amount (PIA) if benefits are not paid before full retirement age.

Non-Participating Provider – Medical providers who reserve the right to charge above the allowable rates set by Medicare. The extra charge, called excess charge, cannot exceed 15% of the Medicare approved amount.

Observation Care – The patient is not admitted but is held in the hospital for observation. Failure to be "admitted" could result in noncoverage of costs by Medicare Part A (Hospital Insurance).

Open Enrollment Period (OEP) – Defines the period of time in which a person eligible for Medicare, Medigap, and prescription coverage can enroll to avoid delays in coverage and possible penalties.

Opt-Out Doctors – Medical providers who do not participate in Medicare.

Original Medicare – Part A (Hospital Insurance) and Part B (Medical Insurance).

Personal Services – A level of care provided to a disabled adult child (child disabled before age 22) who is receiving Social Security benefits. Such services include feeding, bathing, and dressing the disabled adult child. It could also include money management for the disabled adult child.

Premium – Monthly cost for Medicare, Medigap, and prescription drug coverage.

Primary Insurance Amount (PIA) – Amount on which all monthly benefits are determined for retirement, disability, and survivor benefits.

Protective Filing – A protection for the start date of benefits which is established when a person notifies Social Security of an intent to file for benefits. It can protect your entitlement for benefits up to six months in the future for Social Security benefits and up to 60 days for Supplemental Security Income benefits.

Reasonable Charge – The amount that Medicare determines to be an acceptable charge for each type of medical service. Medicare assesses the 20% copay based on the reasonable charge.

Reconsideration – First level of appeal requesting a review of a decision on a claim for Social Security, Supplemental Security Income, and/or Medicare benefits.

Reduction Factor – Monthly percentage that reduces a Social Security benefit before full retirement age.

Reduction Months – Number of months benefits are taken before full retirement age.

Representative Payee – A person appointed by the Social Security Administration to handle the benefits of another person.

Restricted Application – An option available to people born before 1/2/1954 who are eligible for a Spouse's Benefit or Divorced Spouse's Benefit allowing them to receive benefits as a spouse or divorced spouse and delay filing for their own Retirement Benefit.

Retirement Test – The earnings amount allowed before Social Security benefits are affected. The amount usually changes annually.

Retroactivity – Period for which a person is protected for payment of back benefits. For Retirement Benefits, this protection is available only after full retirement age and cannot exceed six months nor precede the month of full retirement age. Disability Benefits can be protected for 12 months of retroactive benefits from the date of application.

Self-employment Income – Net income derived from working for one's self (determined from Schedule C and SE Tax forms).

Special Enrollment Period (SEP) – A period defined by special circumstances that allows a person to delay taking Medicare Parts B, C, D, or Supplemental Medicare during the regular enrollment periods. See pages 79, 80, 85, 88, and 93 respectively.

Special Wage Payment – Remuneration for vacation time, sick time, and/or bonuses based on work for a year prior to retirement. The Special Wage Payment is usually of concern only in the year of retirement and must be verified so that Social Security does not include the Special Wage Payment amount in the total earnings estimate for the Retirement Test.

Totalization Benefit – A benefit that can be payable based on an arrangement between the U.S. and certain foreign countries using work credits from foreign employment. If you have worked under the Social Security program of another country, a determination will be made when you file for benefits regarding the inclusion of earnings from that country.

Wage Earner – Person who worked and earned Social Security credits. Also referred to as the Number Holder and Worker.

Windfall Elimination Provision (WEP) – The Social Security benefit calculation changes to net a lower benefit for someone who is eligible for a pension for which they did not pay Social Security taxes to earn. See example on page 8.

Worksheet Instructions

Trial Work Period & Extended Period of Eligibility

Following are blank worksheets you may photocopy to help you keep track of your Trial Work Period (TWP) months and Substantial Gainful Activity (SGA) months.

The TWP worksheet is designed to cover a 60-month period. Your Trial Work Period expires only after you have used 9 trial work months during a 60-month period. At that point, if you are performing Substantial Gainful Activity (see page 42 for SGA amounts), you will receive two additional months (called your grace period) of Social Security benefits. Benefits will then cease. To review an example on how to complete the TWP worksheet, see pages 45-48.

The Extended Period of Eligibility worksheet will aid you in understanding the Extended Period of Eligibility (EPE). The EPE is a 36-month period that begins the month after your TWP ends. During the EPE, if you have months in which your earnings drop below the SGA level (and you have not had a medical recovery) you might be entitled to benefits for those months. See pages 49-53 for details on how to complete the EPE worksheet.

Note: Copyright Protection:
The Trial Work Period Worksheet and Extended Period of Eligibility Worksheet are under copyright and cannot be printed and distributed. The worksheets are strictly for use by the purchaser of this Social Security-Medicare Guide.

Trial Work Period Worksheet *(See instructions on pp. 45-48)*

	Month & Year of Work	Gross Earnings/ SE Hours	TWP Amounts Allowed	Your TWP Months used	SGA Monthly Amounts	Months with SGA Earnings	SS Benefit Received? Y or N	SS Benefit Due? Y or N
1								
2								
3								
4								
5								
6								
7								
8								
9								
10								
11								
12								
13								
14								
15								
16								
17								
18								
19								
20								
21								
22								
23								
24								
25								
26								
27								
28								
29								

	Month & Year of Work	Gross Earnings/ SE Hours	TWP Amounts Allowed	Your TWP Months used	SGA Monthly Amounts	Months with SGA Earnings	SS Benefit Received? Y or N	SS Benefit Due? Y or N
30								
31								
32								
33								
34								
35								
36								
37								
38								
39								
40								
41								
42								
43								
44								
45								
46								
47								
48								
49								
50								
51								
52								
53								
54								
55								
56								
57								
58								
59								
60								

Extended Period of Eligibility Worksheet *(See instructions on pp. 51-53)*

	Month & Year of Work	SGA Amount Allowed	Your Gross Earnings or SE Hours	Are you due benefits? Y or N
1				
2				
3				
4				
5				
6				
7				
8				
9				
10				
11				
12				
13				
14				
15				
16				
17				
18				
19				
20				
21				
22				
23				
24				
25				
26				
27				
28				
29				

	Month & Year of Work	SGA Amount Allowed	Your Gross Earnings or SE Hours	Are you due benefits? Y or N
30				
31				
32				
33				
34				
35				
36				

Made in the USA
Monee, IL
26 November 2019